J. Lester Brubaker

Cost Accountability

for

School Administrators

Cost Accountability

for

School Administrators

Phillip C. Snyder
Earl E. Hogan

Parker Publishing Company, Inc.   West Nyack, N.Y.

Library of Congress Cataloging in Publication Data

Snyder, Phillip Carl.
   Cost accountability for school administrators.

      1. Schools--Accounting. 2. Education--Costs.
I. Hogan, Earl E.,   joint author. II. Ti-
tle.
LB2830.S52   338.4'3   75-6908
ISBN 0-13-179762-X

Printed in the United States of America

This book is dedicated to our wives
Jo Anna Summers Snyder
and
Mary Webb Hogan
with continuing devotion and love

Dr. Phillip C. Snyder

Dr. Earl E. Hogan

ABOUT THE AUTHORS

Dr. Phillip C. Snyder received his degree in Business and Accounting from Ohio University. His doctoral and post doctoral studies at Ohio U., New York University and Harvard were in Educational Administration and Budgeting, and Finance. He has taught on both Secondary and University levels and served as Superintendent of Schools in Newbury, Ohio.

Dr. Earl E. Hogan has taught on elementary and middle school levels, in addition to teaching at Michigan State where he received his Ph.D. in Administration and curriculum. His experience in public school administration from principal through superintendent in both rural and urban areas contributed to the development of the workable cost account-ability systems described in this book.

The Practical Value of
Cost Accountability System

Today, more than ever before in the history of education, fiscal credibility is being challenged. School administrators are being forced by events and by public opinion to develop comprehensive management information systems. This problem has manifested itself in many ways, including the frequent defeat of tax referendums for school support. In order to present a more productive, credible front, experienced administrators across the nation are looking for planned, organized approaches for improved methods of fiscal reporting.

A cost accountability system is, of course, a necessity in all school systems today. In order to project the idea of credible administrative responsibility with public school systems, school executives are constantly analyzing past techniques of fiscal reporting. The Cost System of Accountability ("CAS") described in this book provides dependable solutions to the many concerns plaguing pupils, teachers, administrators and taxpayers throughout our educational system. For example, it provides a means for analyzing present costs and reorganizing them in a more efficient and effective manner. It allows for a complete analysis of public school expense and develops an accurate relationship between expense and program. "CAS" becomes a workable system, easy to implement and helpful in establishing administrative credibility. As another example, it provides accurate cost figures such as the cost of teaching mathematics at the third grade level or the cost of recess periods at the sixth grade level which have seldom before been available.

This handbook represents a detailed step by step sequence which will allow any school administrator to implement a successful program of cost analysis. Although the design is based, in part, upon a planning, programming, budgeting system approach, in reality, the system is less complicated, more practical, and easier to implement than previous approaches to public school cost analysis. This is because "CAS" starts where you are. The system only requires you to interpret and convert your present accounting system into the simple "CAS" format. It uses your present financial information in a new, more dynamic format which increases it's appeal to faculty and the public. For the first time, school finance will have a more attractive public appearance. This "CAS" system will help you coordinate, far more effectively, the ingredients of curriculum, budget and evaluation which are presently operating within the school system. The system finds its strength in using the specialties of individual staff members and community leaders involved in program development.

A cost accountability system develops out of necessity. The need to provide credible public financial information stimulated the development of "CAS." This same necessity forced the involved administrators to develop a system which was comprehensive, yet simple in structure and implementation. Total involvement is the goal of a credible "CAS" system. This can be accomplished with ease and allows the school administrator to insure the best thinking of his entire constituency. A coordinated system of curriculum decision making allows total personnel involvement.

This system will establish the cost of each program from first grade reading to seventh grade social studies to senior science. An administrator will be able to discuss per pupil cost on the basis of each course offered by the system. For example, these costs will include every expense incurred by the system in the process of offering the course in question. The analysis might determine you are spending $600 each day teaching the pledge to the flag per student while at the same time $60 each day teaching reading at the first grade level. This information can be converted to improved learning, annual reports, public relations releases and Board of Education reports.

This handbook represents six years of concentrated first hand experience in developing a system of accountability which effectively conveys administrative credibility in the turmoil of fiscal chaos resulting from the salary negotiation process forced upon public education today. It provides dynamic financial facts for salary negotiators and community alike which have been nonexistent in the past. These facts will help you decrease expenses by, among other things, combating salary increase demands, and will enable you to increase income by developing greater support for levy campaigns. This "CAS" system can help you sell your public school system to the public it serves.

Phillip C. Snyder, Ph. D.

Earl E. Hogan, Ph. D.

Contents

7. PROJECTING EDUCATIONAL PRIORITIES WITH A FINANCIAL BASE *(Continued)*

8. SELLING EDUCATIONAL PRIORITY ADJUSTMENT TO THE STAFF AND PUBLIC 139

9. STAFF AND PUBLIC INVOLVEMENT IN DEVELOPING CAS 154

Cost Accountability

for

School Administrators

1

Developing the Basis for a Cost Accountability System (CAS)

Support for public education in its most tangible form—financial—has become an increasingly difficult problem for educators at all levels in both public and private institutions. The first warning of this problem came when private institutions felt the squeeze between increased costs of education and decreasing contributions to their cause. This was equally true of public institutions which at the polling place and in the legislature failed to achieve increased support. More recently questions about educational costs and results became explicit with the increasing appearance of reports, articles, books and bulletins all containing, in one way or another, the same recurring theme demanding accountability for educational attainment and costs.

Unfortunately, few educators were ready to answer hard questions when their constituents began to demand educational accountability even when such demands were mandated by the legislature in many states including California and Michigan.

Rather than rise to the challenge, many educators became defensive, made inappropriate statements and indulged in negative action. For example, a local education association in a midwestern state faced with a reduction in teaching force as well as other services in the school district due to repeated failure of millage proposals stated,

"As members of the education profession, we cannot, in good conscience, condone, recommend or initiate any action which would be a step backward in providing quality education for all children."

Most people would agree to that statement, at least in the areas in which they would be affected, but it simply does not face the issue. Indeed, a recent issue of the "School Administrator," official organ of the AASA, indicates this is a national phenomena:

"Prospects appear certain for an overall teacher surplus throughout the 70's and many teachers face the unpleasant prospect of falling victim to a reduction in force. This fact is high in the priorities for local and state teachers' associations. Existing tenure laws furnish little comfort to these leaders. They are being encouraged to impose constraints on boards and administrators at the bargaining tables. Administrators can expect to participate in full-blown public hearings when RIF, as such reductions are being called, is in prospect. Cross examination covering a wide spectrum will be the order of the day."

The public has made its demands and the answers by some educators are anything but satisfactory. In fact, few seem to deal with the very question the public has raised: How can educators be accountable for stewardship of the "talents" which have been entrusted to them by their constituents for education?

CAS: A Dynamic Alternative

Logic leads to the conclusion that there must be some positive, systematic way to approach the problem of accountability. Rather than subjecting all concerned to recrimination, bitterness, misinformation and blaming others, there should be a way of finding out, particularly at the local levels, just where education is, where it is going and how it is going to get there.

For some educators, increasing public school expenditures and demands for an accounting led to a search for a positive system to aid them in a more effective and efficient way to use allocated resources and to find answers to questions being raised about their use. Their search led them beyond what educators have been able to report over the years: the per pupil, per bus and per route costs of transporting pupils, or the cost of cleaning, heating and maintaining a school building, or feeding a child. Their search led to ways to answer questions about what it costs to raise a child's reading or computation skills to a higher level. For example, what happens if more or less is spent to achieve a new level of learning in a longer or shorter time? How can this be communicated to the taxpayers in relation to cost?

They recognized a need for a more responsive and timely cost accountability system that effectively communicates the cost of educational output. They needed a cost accountability system that would allow for better decision making, alternative selection, planning and forecasting.

One dynamic practical system is called CAS, and it appears capable of meeting these needs.

What Is CAS?

CAS is a synthesis of established techniques that are applied to management and control processes to produce a budget that relates to the output activities in an organization and further relates it to input resources. There are many advantages to CAS, but one of the major ones is that the outputs of the programs of the school are measured and emphasized, rather than the inputs or resources necessary to support them. Another outstanding value of CAS is its ability to provide an uncomplicated and logical beginning for even the smallest school district.

Its value results from an integrated practical system of components to provide those using CAS the information for continued better educational decision making and analysis. With this system, educational institutional staffs have better means for planning educational programs and for making choices among the alternative ways to which funds can be allocated to achieve the school district's established objectives, the programs to reach these objectives, the methods of evaluating the programs and the costs of operating them. In essence, rather than the defensive self defeating statement "give us more money and we will produce the results," the CAS response is "Having evaluated and thoroughly analyzed what we are currently spending and its allocation, by re-allocation we can do these things. However, given more resources we can do these additional things also."

The analysis and evaluation central to the implementation of CAS requires identification of the end products. Current processes are analyzed first, then alternate ways are considered for meeting and finding objectives through utilization of various combinations of personnel, facilities and material to bring about the desired educational results. The important question, repeatedly asked with increasing sophistication to provide answers regarding the use of CAS, is how much additionally would be gained or lost by way of achieving the defined objectives through spending more or less for the purpose.

The purpose of this book is to help you gain increasing ability to develop such a system in your educational organization.

The Language of CAS

To better understand CAS, we must first develop some common ground based upon the organization and terminology used in this management system.

The elements of CAS can be organized in several ways. However, it is a complete system capable of incorporating means whereby simple as well as complex curriculum, financial and evaluation analysis can be welded together as an entity which supports and enhances decisions made in any of those three areas. To achieve this goal, CAS is more commonly categorized as goals, objectives, programs (curriculum), budgeting, operation (financial analysis) and evaluation (educational results). Illus. 1-1 illustrates these components and their relationships.

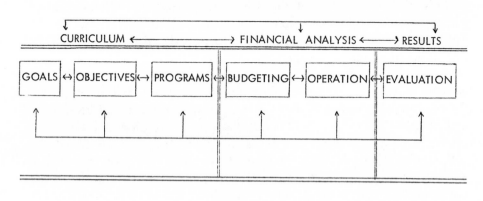

Illus. 1-1

Goals are general statements of purpose. They are not related to a specific period of time, are not quantifiable or measurable except in a broad subjective manner, and ideally should be defined in terms of a broad base of community need.

Objectives represent measurable achievement, attainment of which advances a school system in the direction of established goals. Objectives stem directly from one or more of the goals. Objectives can be defined as desirable quantifiable accomplishments within a specific time framework.

Programs are groups of interrelated activities directed toward accomplishing objectives. Budgeting presents financial data for existing and alternative programs projected annually, as well as over several years.

Operations is what it indicates—the actual operations of the program and the management of the resources to implement them. Evaluation is the process whereby the effectiveness of the program operations is measured against the criteria established earlier in the objectives.

Budgeting: Tells It Like It Is

Illus. 1-1 shows the classical approach to developing a cost accountability system. If the time, resources, manpower and commitment are present this is the ideal way to approach such a project. The CAS system fosters and accommodates such an approach. However, most educational institutions are not in a position to approach a project in this manner. In fact, many educators have been discouraged, or have abandoned their efforts, when faced by the technical language and confusing accounting patterns inherent with detailed financial analysis that is emphasized by other approaches. Others have had difficulties accommodating state required or existing function-object accounting methods to a program budget approach.

To overcome these problems, CAS incorporates management systems generally called program budgeting and program cost accounting as a starting point for a CAS system for educational institutions. Such an approach permits a portrayal of the educational institution's expenditures in terms of programs and permits the institutional personnel to raise questions about program interest and allocation of such resources. It also provides administrators, board members, staff and the community with a clear explanation of how tax dollars are being spent; thus being able to produce positive, direct information for all these groups for educational decision making.

This approach also does not interfere with the usual function-object accounting system and procedures of an educational institution, but enhances such a system.

Illus. 1-2 depicts the manner in which a typical state mandated function-object budget in a middle size school district can continue to operate and be accommodated by the CAS program approach for the same district.

BUDGETING CONTRASTS

Function-Object Budget		Program Budget	
Instruction	$ 9,353,200	Art	$ 652,600
Administration	420,800	Business Education	331,500
Health and Nursing	36,700	Community Service	24,700
Transportation	374,700	Driver Education	20,800
Operation	1,489,500	Foreign Language	209,300
Maintenance	405,000	Home Economics	295,100
Fixed Charges	681,500	Industrial Education	393,900
Capital Outlay	84,100	Kindergarten	455,000
Community Services	26,000	Language Arts	3,108,300
Student Services	6,000	Mathematics	1,723,800
Athletics	120,000	Multi-Media	430,300
Outgoing Transfers		Music	544,700
Tuition	2,500	Physical Education	685,100
		Pupil Personnel Services	835,900
		Reading Improvement	418,600
	$ 13,000,000	School Farm	15,600
		Science	1,072,500
		Social Studies	1,426,100
		Vocational Education	356,200
			$ 13,000,000

Illus. 1-2

Illus. 1-2 and 1-3 portray in clear terms the added dimensions of information available to educators through CAS as they concern themselves with present and future planning of their district.

Further, when developing the budget in relation to the program, it is possible in the CAS approach to reach some decisions by looking at the amount of dollars being spent. This would reveal just what the objectives and goals in the school system actually are. For example, in school districts using program analysis, when all costs of the language arts program were considered, they were unaware that about one-third of the total school operating budget is spent on this particular program. Generally, the second most expensive program will be mathematics.

Illus. 1-3 portrays such a relationship of program to budget, goal, and objectives in the school district analyzed in Illus. 1-2. Clearly, the major goals and objectives of this school system lie first in the language arts area, and second in mathematics. This logical approach, coupled with estimates and derived formulas, which will be explained fully in later chapters, is a simplified, practical method of approaching goals and objectives. In essence it says "what you spend is what you are," and through budget analysis based upon programs, educational institutions enter into a consideration of their goals and objectives with no preconceived notions.

As skill is gained with annual and multi-year program accounting and budgeting, the educational institution, over a period of years, will want to develop budgeting and spending more directly related to goals, objectives and evaluations, as these CAS components and their interrelationships, as shown in Illus. 1-1, are more clearly defined. Such developments will come with use of the CAS system at the pace and to the depth desired, and within the resources allocated by those concerned with the operation of the school or institution.

Goals: Bench Marks of Education

Armed with the information derived through CAS program budget accounting methods, the school staff and community can return their attention to a further analysis of this vital component of the CAS system.

In establishing goals, the needs of the community should be identified further and compared with previous statements and CAS findings. The needs of the children, adults, business and industry, other governmental units, etc., and as far as possible, all the elements of the community's needs, should be brought together and translated into goals or general statements of purpose or intent.

Such goals should be arranged in a logical structure displaying the broadest high level goals in relation to the more specific lower level goals

PROGRAM PRIORITIES

5%	10%	15%	20%	25%	30%

Language Arts
Mathematics
Social Studies
Science
Pupil Personnel Services
Physical Education
Art
Music
Kindergarten
Multi-Media
Reading Improvement
Industrial Education
Vocational Education
Business Education
Home Economics
Foreign Language
Community Service
Driver Education
School Farm

% of Total
Budget

PROGRAM	% OF TOTAL	AMOUNT BUDGETED
Art	5.0	$ 652,600
Business Education	2.6	331,500
Community Service	.2	24,700
Driver Education	.2	20,800
Foreign Language	1.6	209,300
Home Economics	2.3	295,100
Industrial Education	3.0	393,900
Kindergarten	3.5	455,000
Language Arts	23.9	3,108,300
Mathematics	13.3	1,723,800
Multi-Media	3.3	430,300
Music	4.2	544,700
Physical Education	5.3	685,100
Pupil Personnel Services	6.4	835,900
Reading Improvement	3.2	418,600
School Farm	.1	15,600
Science	8.3	1,072,500
Social Studies	11.0	1,426,100
Vocational Education	2.7	356,200

RANK ORDER OF PROGRAMS

Illus. 1-3

that support them, and should show their direct relationship to the objectives that carry them out. A typical goal structure is shown in Illus. 1-4 as G1 through G4.

CAS GOAL AND OBJECTIVE ANALYSIS

G1   To provide for all students the opportunity to develop skills and characteristics enabling them to gain employment.

     01 For 90 percent of the graduating seniors that wish to enter the labor force to gain employment in business within three months of graduation as measured by a district survey.

G2   To provide for all students the opportunity to develop skills and characteristics in business, industrial arts, agriculture.

     02 For 90 percent of the graduating seniors that wish to enter the labor force to gain employment as desired in business, industrial arts and agriculture within three months of graduation as measured by a district survey.

G3   To provide for all students the opportunity to develop skills and characteristics in typing, shorthand, bookkeeping and office machine operation.

     03 For 90 percent of the business curriculum students to meet the following standards:

        03.1 Typing—40 words per minute as measured by the IBM test with 90 percent accuracy.

        03.2 Shorthand—60 words per minute as measured by the Gregg test with a 2,000 word vocabulary.

        03.3 Bookkeeping—demonstrate understanding of journals, income statements and balance sheets as determined by classroom tests.

        03.4 Office Machine Operation—mean score equal to national average on NCR tests.

G4   To provide for all students the opportunity to develop skills and characteristics in bookkeeping.

     04 Upon course completion 90 percent of students will be able to accomplish the following based on classroom tests:

        04.1 State and understand the basic accounting equation of double entry bookkeeping.

        04.2 Understand the function of and make journal entries.

        04.3 Understand three depreciation calculation methods.

Illus. 1-4

Objectives: Action Analysis

Objectives bring life to community goals and have a typical structure:

1. Relate to one or more goals.

2. Are measurable.
3. State method of measurement.
4. Indicate the criteria for evaluation.
5. State the time period for obtaining the objective.

A highly sophisticated, complex, but extremely useful approach to educational objectives has been organized by Bloom and others in *A Taxonomy of Educational Objectives–Handbooks I and II*. An example of the practical application of their work can be found in Mager's *Preparing Educational Objectives*.

In a CAS analysis, goals are translated into realistic, action filled specific activities that are understandable to both staff and community.

When goals described in Illus. 1-4 are subjected to CAS analysis, they take on the form and substance shown as 01 through 04 in Illus. 1-4. Note that their components are statements of ordinary practice with readily available, commonly used tests, or are easily followed up by a guidance department.

Such use of readily available, familiar practices and procedures, recombined in a systematic, related way, is the hallmark of the CAS approach.

CAS, for example, also permits a simple, realistic beginning approach to developing objectives by use of the table of contents of textbooks adopted by a school system. This is probably the best statement of curricular objectives readily available in a school system or educational institution. Further, by simply restating the table of contents in behavioral terms, as some textbook publishers have already done, one can reach a beginning level of constructing and organizing curriculum and objectives by a staff with something they understand and with which they are familiar. One certainly would not want to remain at such a beginning level. However, getting started is important, and such an approach supplies an excellent beginning and a point of departure.

It should be observed that the objectives in Illus. 1-4 contain within them one or more evaluative criteria. Inherent in any good set of objectives are the evaluative criteria by which the effectiveness of the program objectives will be measured. Each objective contains such criteria for measurement and evaluation. Measuring program effectiveness is one of the most difficult problems encountered in the development of most management systems. Very few, if any, systems and procedures are established in school districts for measurement, other than the standardized test for measuring performance of broad basic educational areas for such things as computational skills in mathematics, or comprehension in reading. However, the CAS system recognizes that such criteria and systems for evaluation, if they are at all organized, can provide the basis for developing a CAS analysis of the evaluation component shown in Illus. 1-1.

At the other extreme, one should keep in mind that there are some subjective areas of the educational process which probably cannot be evaluated quantitatively. However, when this is accepted as true, it should be stated explicitly in such form as "teacher's opinion," or whatever the method of criteria being used as subjective evaluation of the objective.

Although difficult to quantify, there is general agreement among educators that evaluation criteria in the subjective areas is necessary and must be developed. CAS holds the promise of aiding educators and psychologists to begin such a breakthrough.

Program's Carry Out the Goals and Objectives

When goals and objectives have been defined, the next step is to decide what programs will attain the objectives. As previously defined, a program is simply a group of interrelated activities directed toward accomplishing objectives. Programs should be arranged in a structure that shows a relationship to the objectives and goals. For CAS, analysis programs in most school districts are the basic educational areas referred to in Illus. 1-3, such as language arts, science, mathematics, music, social studies, etc., and others such as learning resource centers, driver education, or perhaps outdoor education.

Usually, no formal statement covering the programs of the educational institution exists. Minor rearrangements of the existing textbook, curriculum guide or subject outline will usually provide the basis for program structures within the basic educational disciplines. Eventually, each educational institution will decide for itself what programs make sense to it, and devise an organizational program pattern which explains its activities as the school district in Illus. 1-3 and 1-4 has done.

The major criteria is the need to define and organize programs so that they are explicit and are useful to those involved. For CAS purposes, programs should be analyzed by major program area or parts of that major area, and should eventually present alternatives, recommendations and cost estimates extending over the anticipated life of the program in an organized written form. When that level of analysis has been achieved, alternative programs can be examined, and modification to the present program can be considered in light of the financial and resource limitations.

Evaluation: Tells It Like It Is

The final step in the development of CAS has been discussed in some detail in relation to objectives. The evaluation cycle should describe the effectiveness of the program operation against the criteria established for the various program objectives. The process then recycles (see Illus. 1-1) such evaluation information to determine whether objectives are attained or not. Analysis, no matter how rudimentary, based upon evaluation is quite important, since resources are limited and any direction of programs based upon evaluative information is always more productive and explicit.

CAS is a continually active process which requires that current programs or activities be subjected to periodic analysis, and that these programs be continued, modified or eliminated from the system. The replacements are chosen from alternatives, and they in turn are subjected to the same analysis.

The Promise of CAS

In today's world, educators are subject to competition for financing by many groups. When challenged to offer hard evidence of wise use of funds and to reveal results from past and present costs and efforts, many realize they don't really know what it costs to educate the children in their district or how to go about finding out. Many have been faced with the necessity of having to cut a budget or face a reduction in force, and have been frustrated by the lack of information about what to trim first. They often have been forced to consider recommendations for new school programs without supporting information on alternative programs, costs and probable benefits. CAS holds the promise of providing answers to these problems.

CAS is as complicated as you choose to make it, but in any form it can make decision and policy making a much more systematic and intelligent process. CAS identifies alternative ways of achieving a given end and developing information necessary for making choices among alternatives. If properly implemented, it is possible to conduct the public's business faster, better and at a minimum cost. CAS is beginning to be used by an ever increasing group of institutions, and its benefits have been quite impressive.

CAS must begin with the adoption of a cost accounting system quite different from today's school accounting process. In traditional school accounting, expenditures are grouped together by function and object. For example, all administrative costs are lumped into one major account. All instructional costs are kept separate. No attempt is made to determine the cost of a particular program or activity, such as allocating to it a certain portion of the administrative cost, and so on. Because of this approach, individual costs of many programs in nearly all school districts today are not known and cannot be determined without a great deal of time, effort and headache. The function-object accounting system used by most educational institutions has been around since shortly after the turn of the century, and has served its purpose well during an era when school districts were smaller, educational programs less complex, and competition for the tax dollar was less intense. Although the emphasis of CAS is clearly upon program costs, CAS is sophisticated enough to provide data in any meaningful array desired.

CAS has many advantages. It can help schools begin at various levels of sophistication to:

1. Improve cost analysis as a control.
2. Evaluate programs in terms of objectives, costs and benefits.
3. Identify and analyze alternative ways of achieving the same goal.
4. Establish priorities.
5. Allocate resources in light of total needs and resources.
6. Praise the performance of those responsible for reaching stated goals.
7. Coordinate short range and long range planning, and
8. Inform the public of the purposes, costs and expected results of the schools' programs.

CAS has its disadvantages also:

1. It takes time, money and skill to fully develop and operate.
2. It can result in more detailed accounting and budgeting documents requiring summarizations and interpretations.
3. It may result in placement of too much emphasis on the cost of the programs rather than on their benefits.
4. It may meet with resistance from staff members who resent the systemization of the education process.

Finally, CAS is so promising that no school district should overlook its potential. Certainly, districts even without data processing capabilities should be moving toward the CAS system with all deliberate speed. At the very minimum, districts should be doing some preliminary work on a CAS system, and pushing for establishment of statewide and national guidelines for this new approach to school accounting.

Beyond this, whatever can be accomplished in the way of more clearly defining district programs, their goals and objectives, and assigning a dollar amount to them, will put the district a long way down the road toward a better management information system and decision making process in your educational institution—which is what CAS is all about!

2

How to Display Current Budgets As Individual District Programs

Your Present Budget

Most school administrators are familiar with the line item type of budgetary organization. Each state mandates that Boards of Education develop their budgetary and fiscal arrangements on a predetermined line item basis. These accounts are dictated by the state as a method of developing uniformity in the appropriations and budgeting documents of the individual school districts. Some typical budgetary divisions found in line item budgets are administration, instruction, coordinate activities, libraries, transportation of pupils, recreational activities, auxiliary agencies and capital outlay.

Positive Program Titles

As a result of these state mandated listings of accounts, the typical school administrator is restricted in his presentation of a financial picture of his school district. In order to escape the restrictions of the line item format for budgetary appropriations, it is necessary to translate this format into a list of programs. These programs represent the actual courses taught in the school system, which make up the curricular offerings for students. The first step to the development of a program listing of courses with a school district is the identification of the various program divisions presently offered within the system. For example, all school systems have a reading program; some include this reading program as part of the total language arts program. All school systems have a social studies program. These are examples of types of programs found in typical school systems. Illus. 2-1 shows a line item budget. It shows how a school system's fiscal spending can be appropriated in terms of the line item accounts. Illus. 2-2 is a breakdown of subject matter accounts, based upon the subject of a particular school system. Notice that the totals of both Illus. 2-1 and Illus. 2-2 are identical; however, the breakdowns of spending between these two are characteristically different. Herein lies the secret and the value of a program budgeting system.

The determination of course descriptions or program titles is a simple, uncomplex process. All that is needed is a copy of the current course offerings at the secondary level. By taking these course offerings and listing them, you will soon discover that you have between eighteen and twenty-five course offerings within your school district. Usually, the course offerings at the secondary level are extensions of the course offerings at the elementary level. Therefore, only in cases such as kindergarten is it necessary to itemize or list elementary course offerings separately. The obvious advantage to listing fiscal spending in this manner is that the division categories are related to instructional programs typically existing within the school system. For example, most taxpayers realize that every school system has a social studies program or a mathematics program. However, when they read that the total cost of the transportation of pupils or coordinate activities is a number of dollars, there is doubt in their minds as to exactly how accountable the school system is with regard to spending tax money.

STATE MANDATED LISTING OF THE
PROJECTED APPROPRIATIONS FOR THE 19-- FISCAL YEAR

	LINE ITEM	AMOUNT APPROPRIATED
1.	Administration	$ 135,713.00
2.	Instruction	2,047,160.00
3.	Coordinate Activities	68,617.00
4.	Libraries	43,043.00
5.	Transportation of Pupils	94,400.00
6.	Recreational Activities	7,000.00
7.	Auxiliary Agencies	453,500.00
8.	Operation of School Plant	371,692.00
9.	Maintenance of School Plant	45,116.00
10.	Capital Outlay	11,100.00
11.	Federal Programs	98,000.00
	TOTAL PROJECTED 19-- APPROPRIATIONS	$3,375,341.00

Illus. 2-1

The above state mandated budgetary listing is difficult to understand because the division categories are unrelated to the instructional programs typically existing within Anytown and other school districts.

ANYTOWN SCHOOLS' COST ACCOUNTABILITY SYSTEM

LISTING OF THE 19-- PROJECTED APPROPRIATIONS

PROGRAMS BY SUBJECT	AMOUNT APPROPRIATED
1. Vocational Agriculture	$ 11,936.74
2. Art	128,458.98
3. Business Education	95,493.96
4. Learning Resource Centers	46,435.24
5. Language Arts	1,029,052.45
6. Foreign Language	54,324.00
7. Physical Education	170,581.72
8. Home Economics	59,683.73
9. Industrial Arts	60,309.03
10. Mathematics	351,009.33
11. Music	123,520.79
12. Science and Health	315,951.28
13. Social Studies	310,947.56
14. Student Activities (Sports, etc.)	51,246.97
15. Coordination (Includes classroom administration)	238,702.20
16. Child Study Center	226,240.93
17. Kindergarten	89,509.25
18. Driver Education	11,936.74
TOTAL PROJECTED 19-- APPROPRIATIONS	$3,375,341.00

This listing of costs shows the projected expense of maintaining the above subject matter areas for the 19-- Fiscal Year. (From January 1, 19-- to December 31, 19--.)

Item fifteen, Coordination, includes the percentage of each teacher's salary which pays for lunch money collecting, attendance taking, and record keeping within each classroom, as well as all other administrative expenses related to normal operation. Also, the administrative costs for the Kindergarten Program are included under item fifteen, Coordination.

Ninety per cent (90%) of our Kindergarten Program cost is paid for from state support, the other ten per cent (10%) is paid for from local taxes.

Illus. 2-2

It is important to include all course titles under programs. It is possible, such as in the case of language arts, to include reading, writing, spelling and English under one program or subject title. However, whatever program title you use, be sure that you cover all expenditures within the school system under some program title listed. Administration within the school system deserves special attention. Some school systems include all administrative costs under the title Program Coordination. This is listed as a separate program in the program budget listing for the system. Program coordination, of course, includes all buildings, central office administrators and a portion of each classroom teacher's time—that portion, of course, which that classroom teacher uses to make attendance, fill out grade records and perform other administrative functions within the classroom. Now that we have both an understanding of the state mandated listings for appropriation documents, those which we have referred to as line items, and a complete understanding of programs by subject matter offered in the school system, normally referred to as course offerings, we can move on to "how" or "what" connection exists between these two concepts of budgeting and appropriations.

Crosswalk Concept

The next concept to be discussed with regard to implementing an accountability system is the "Crosswalk Concept." This system utilizes a traditional accounting format, listing horizontally the various line items and totals in your present appropriations or budgeting document. Vertically down the side of the "crosswalk" it is necessary to list the programs which you have identified as being descriptive of the programs actually offered by your school system. The next step, of course, is to fill in the blanks which exist under each of the line items within your budget. The total of this "crosswalk" is considered the total of your appropriations or budgeting fiscal responsibilities. (See Illus. 2-3) It is important here to realize that the "crosswalk" represents only an approximation of the spending in each category represented. These approximations are arrived at through a series of mathematical calculations which determine the validity of the figures appropriated. Herein lies the importance and the accuracy of your accountability system. Careful calculation of the "crosswalk" and careful preparation of the representative totals insures validity and reliability with regard to your final accountability breakdown. Once the "crosswalk" from Level I, your line item budget, to Level II, your program determination budget, is completed, and the "crosswalk" has been determined, you can utilize the figures arrived at in many different ways. At this point in the determination of your accountability system, you will have certain facts at your disposal which have never been available to you as a school administrator before. For example, you will know the total cost of your present art program, kindergarten through the twelfth grade level. You will be able to determine the total cost of your mathematics program or music program or, for that matter, any other program which exists within your school system as a individual entity. As a progressive, conscientious school administrator, you can see the obvious advantages of having these figures at your immediate disposal. For example, if it's necessary for you to approximate appropriations for the following school year, your accuracy will improve by adding the inflationary factor to each of your individual program breakdown figures, thus representing a new appropriations document for the following year on the Level II basis. You may, at your discretion, use Level II as a quick, ready reference to your state mandated line item appropriations. Thus you have a ready reference to analyze the previous breakdown utilized in your financial documents. Relationships between line item accounts such as transportation and program accounts such as science and health become obvious. Many relationships never before included in public school financial documents are now clearly visible. You can determine how much it costs to transport students for your art program or your vocational agriculture program. It is obvious how much your maintenance cost is for your home economics program or your foreign language program. These are rather revolutionary concepts in terms of analyzing school spending. However, remember we are striving to understand the complexities of the spending of large amounts of capital on many diversified programs involving many variables. Although the goals of our "CAS" are diverse and complex in their conception, it is apparent that a basic, uncomplex approach toward financial divisions within our budgetary system allows us an easy, quick reference to understanding our fiscal policies.

COST ACCOUNTABILITY SYSTEM
LEVEL I AND LEVEL II BREAKDOWN

Level II / Level I	Admin. 135,713.	- Line Items - Instr. 1,780.000.	Libraries 43,043.	Buses 130,460.
Programs:				
1. Vocational Agr.	297.			
2. Art	3,198.			
3. Business Educ.	2,377.			
4. Language Arts	25,591.			
5. Science & Health	7,851.			
10.				

Illus. 2-3
The "Crosswalk Concept"[1]

---

[1]The "Crosswalk Concept" allows to redistribute line item costs to program costs.

How to Utilize the Crosswalk

Your financial "crosswalk," moving you from your line item budget to your program accounts, offers a wide variety of utilizations for disseminating information concerning your fiscal spending. Use this information to compare costs of various programs within the school system. Also use this information to illustrate the value of your spending in relation to student achievement.

Formation of Breakdown Formulas

In the process of developing a formula breakdown for the conversion of your fiscal system from Level I to Level II, it is necessary to first determine a common unit of analysis. At this point, you may use one of two basic units for your calculations. Some school systems use an average teacher's salary for determining their unit of comparison. If this is done, simply take your entire payroll for the school year and divide it by the number of teachers, thus giving you the average teacher's salary within the school district. If you chose to use a student unit of measure as the calculating factor, obviously, you would take the total expenditures of the school system and divide them by the total number of students in the school system, giving you a per pupil unit cost for management within the school system. It is our opinion that the more accurate figure would be the teacher unit comparison. Therefore, our calculations and illustrations are based upon an average teacher unit as determined by the above method. (See Illus. 2-4)

PROGRAM UNIT COST BREAKDOWN

Example:

Average teacher's salary $5,000

Total cost of all school system programs $100,000

Program:
Language Arts   = 4 teacher units
Mathematics   = 2 teacher units

Breakdown Formula:

Illus. 2-4

Program: Language Arts

Step 1:   Teacher Units × Average Teachers Salary = Unit Cost of Program

Step 2:   Total Program Cost ÷ Unit Cost of Program = Percentage of Total
Cost Represented by Program.

Example—Language Arts:
   4 × \$5,000 = \$20,000

   \$20,000 ÷ \$100,000 = 20%

Illus. 2-4 *(Con't.)*

Accurate Calculations

Once the average unit is determined as a factor for comparative analysis and financial spending, it is a very simple task to interpret each program in Level II with respect to the number of teachers that that program represents. For example, if you have a business education program, which involves eight teachers, then in terms of teacher units, that business education program would be interpreted as eight parts. A language arts program, which includes kindergarten through the twelfth grade students, involves more units than, say, a program at the eleventh grade such as mathematics, which may only involve a small number of units. Once each program within the school program has been interpreted in terms of common teacher units, then it is necessary to determine the percentage of total teacher units within the system represented by that particular program. For example, if you had a program such as mathematics which was represented by ten teacher units, and you had a total of one hundred teacher units within the school system, then that mathematics program would represent one-tenth or 10 percent of the total cost of your school system.

Margin of Error

As you can see, it is a very uncomplex procedure to develop programs in terms of teacher units and to interpret those costs in terms of percentages. However, it is necessary to keep in mind that all of these calculations are subject to a certain margin of error. Normally, if the average teacher unit is calculated accurately, in terms of total spending, then the margin of error will not exceed 5 percent. In extreme cases where a program actually exceeds the cost of an average teacher unit, it might be necessary to weigh that program in order to determine an exact cost. For example, you might have one teacher teaching in a remote area, such as vocational agriculture, and if that teacher is a high salaried teacher, he will cost the school system more funds than what an average teacher unit would represent. However, any financial weighting which you apply toward determining your fiscal position should be done after the total program accountability breakdown is complete. In most cases, weighting is not necessary; and even when weighting will improve the accuracy of the original breakdown, the advantages arrived at through the weighting process are doubtful. Thus, in many cases, weighting represents the disadvantage of having an uncoordinated, illogical financial picture as opposed to a logically determined, consistent breakdown.

Effect of Weighting

In general, as you develop the breakdown formulas and the rationale for the description of programs within the school system, maintain consistency, develop accuracy and allow for a 5 percent error which results from not weighting the programs representing experience and preparation within the school district. By determining the percentage which each program represents of the total funds developed within the school district, it is possible to break down each line item into the program which it represents on the "crosswalk" as determined through the accountability process. (See Illus. 2-3 and Illus. 2-4)

In examining the Level II breakdown formulas, (see Illus. 2-4), there are cases where special teachers are used to support a program, and a portion of each special teacher's time is figured into the overall percentage of teachers representing that particular program. For example, if 5 percent of each of your elementary teacher's time is used to support the physical education program at each grade level, kindergarten through sixth, then this percentage of time must be figured into the total number of teacher units representing that program. In terms of some programs, such as mathematics, probably a 15 percent figure would be more accurate in terms of estimating the elementary teacher's time involved in that program. All percentages could most accurately be arrived at through a determination of time spent by each individual teacher carrying out the responsibilities required by that particular subject area. Most states have developed timetables or time charts which represent the recommended amount of time to be utilized by each teacher within a subject matter area. These time charts or schedules become rational, foundational bases for determining percentages which represent that particular program within the total fiscal accountability system.

Presenting Dynamic Results

All of these percentages should be arrived at independent of the program, and then applied to the instructional program in terms of average teacher units. Once the total number of average teacher units has been determined for each instructional area, then it is only necessary to divide the average teacher units into the total number of teacher units to determine the percentage of funding which applies to that particular program. Once these percentages are arrived at within a school system, they will not change from year to year, unless the staffing patterns change. For example, if you employ ten teachers in the area of mathematics during this school year and next year you employ twelve, then the percentage of funding represented by that particular program will change proportionately. However, if no change in staffing occurs from one year to another, then it is equally true that the percentage of funding will not fluctuate. Although these facts are hidden realizations, which are actualized as a result of a consistent approach to responsible fiscal planning, they represent accuracy in terms of spending for programs within the school system. Our goal is to represent our spending and our pattern of financial management in terms of student needs and eventual student achievement. The first, and most logical, step to itemizing fiscal spending in terms of actual dollars is an accurate breakdown of programs within the school system in terms of average teacher units applied to those programs. Once this has been accomplished, it is a relatively simple matter to apply these findings in a comparison with the achievement evidenced within the various instructional programs by measuring this achievement through standardized tests, designed for this purpose. As we progress through the development of our fiscal plan, it will become more and more obvious that the fallibility which is inherent within the available measuring instruments becomes also a limitation of this system.

The argument which seems to be paramount in terms of defending the logic of the basic "CAS" approach is the same logic which defends the fallibility of available instructional measurement instruments within our society. If a test has been determined to be 93 percent valid in the eyes of expert academicians, then who are we to question its validity as we apply instructional costs to it? Our purpose is not to rediscover the wheel; moreover, our purpose is to apply a sound, rational approach to financial spending and to interpret our financial spending in an acceptable, rational way for public consumption. If your process helps to convince taxpayers that their money is well spent and well managed, then we have achieved our purpose. At the same time, our facts and figures can contribute to improving our appropriations documents and the accuracy with which we present them to Boards of Education for approval. These are admirable goals and long overdue in terms of determining fiscal responsibility and financial credibility for school systems throughout our nation. To confuse the purpose of our project is to accomplish nothing. Therefore, we submit that any fallibility or error of calculation which exists must be represented by the validity of the measuring instruments which are used. These applications represent the possible utilization of the results at the Level II area of accountability determination.

Information, Personnel and Equipment Needed to Succeed

At this point it is essential that subordinate administrators, principals, and the staff in general be oriented to the purpose of the "CAS" System. Additional electronic calculators will be needed along with the following information. This may be accomplished through a series of in-system seminars designed to explain all details of the CAS process.

A complete description of line items, codes, and description presently being used in the school system.

LEVEL I—COORDINATE ACTIVITIES

Personal Services:

A-17	Attendance Officer
A-20	Nurses
A-21	Counselors

LEVEL I—LIBRARIES

Personal Services:

A-22	Library Employees

Other Expenses:

B-5	Library Books—Secondary
B-5e	Library Books—Elementary

LEVEL I—TRANSPORTATION OF PUPILS

Personal Services:

A-23	Bus Drivers

Other Expenses:

B-2	Supplies for Motor Vehicles
C-3	Materials for Maintenance
D-2	Equipment Replacement
E-4	Contract, Repair

Illus. 2-5

A coded listing of all instructional programs presently in operation in the school district.

LEVEL II–PROGRAM

CODE
01	Vocational Agriculture
02	Art
03	Business Education
04	Learning Resource Centers
05	Language Arts (Including English)
06	Foreign Language
07	
08	Physical Education
09	Home Economics
10	Industrial Arts
11	Mathematics
12	Music
13	Science & Health
14	Plant Maintenance
15	Social Studies
16	Plant Operation
17	Student Activities (Football, etc.)
18	Program Administration
19	Child Study Center (Including All Services)
20	Transportation, Teachers
21	Kindergarten
22	
30	Driver Education

Illus. 2-6

A PRIORITY LISTING OF PROGRAMS
ACCORDING TO TOTAL COST

Level II

Program Code	Rank	Level II Program	Total Cost
05	1	Language Arts	$1,029,052.45
11	2	Mathematics	351,009.33
13	3	Science and Health	315,951.28
15	4	Social Studies	310,947.56

Illus. 2-7

18	5	Program Administration	238,702.20
19	6	Child Study Center	226,240.93
08	7	Physical Education	170,581.72
02	8	Art	128,458.98
12	9	Music	123,520.79
03	10	Business Education	95,493.96
21	11	Kindergarten	89,509.25
10	12	Industrial Arts	60,309.03
09	13	Home Economics	59,683.73
06	14	Foreign Language	54,324.00
17	15	Student Activities	51,246.97
04	16	Learning Resource Centers	46,435.24
30	17	Driver Education	11,936.74
01	18	Vocational Agriculture	11,936.74

Illus. 2-7 *(Con't.)*

A PRIORITY LISTING OF PROGRAMS
ACCORDING TO PER PUPIL COST

Program Code	Rank	Level II Program	Total Cost
21	1	Kindergarten	$208.16
05	2	Language Arts	207.05
01	3	Vocational Agriculture	205.81
03	4	Business Education	163.80
18	5	Foreign Language	126.93
30	6	Driver Education	94.74
11	7	Math	87.91
09	8	Home Economics	86.62
10	9	Industrial Arts	84.70
13	10	Science & Health	79.13

Illus. 2-8

15	11	Social Studies	71.16
18	12	Program Administration	44.20
19	13	Child Study Center	41.90
08	14	Physical Education	39.95
02	15	Art	35.98
12	16	Music	31.71
04	17	Learning Resource Centers	20.19
17	18	Student Activities	9.49

Illus. 2-8 *(Con't.)*

LEVEL I TO LEVEL II
CONVERSION FORMULA PERCENTAGES
BY PROGRAM

Program	Percentage Applied
1. Art	.039
2. Program (Atten. Records, Grades, Etc.)	.051
3. Business Education	.029
4. Driver Education	.004
5. Foreign Language	.016
6. Home Economics	.030
7. Industrial Arts	.018
8. Kindergarten	.027
9. Language Arts	.238
10. Mathematics	.110
11. Library	.022
12. Music	.038
13. Physical Education	.051
14. Distributive Education	.038
15. Science & Health	.090
16. Social Studies	.080
17. Student Activities	.015
18. Machine Shop	.048
19. E.M.R. Program	.056
	1.000

Illus. 2-9

3

Effective Techniques for Presenting Accurate Building Expense

Part of the value of an accurate cost accountability system is its utilization and effectiveness in developing a concise and accurate building level cost breakdown. In Chapter 2, the program cost analysis was discussed. However, to be completely effective, the program costs must be interpreted at the building level. Developing building costs involves an understanding of the utilization of all factors contributing to the overall production of education. These factors of course include labor, in the form of teaching personnel; materials, in the form of textbooks and other teaching devices; and classroom space or working area. Our goal in this chapter is to develop a logical progression in the overall analysis of our financial situation by first determining the extent of use of each of the factors responsible for the production of education within our system. Then we will apply these various ratios to the costs which are incurred in the process of arriving at our objectives. In order to do this, it is essential that we understand the complexity of the problem with which we are involved.

Creating Building Budget Concepts

Let us, for example, consider some of the factors and influence present within a school system. Rhetorically, how much do we know about the cost of operating the individual building? Most financial managers determine building costs by merely adding up the various costs which are incurred during the normal fiscal period. Although this gives us certain information, it is not an accurate cost analysis for the production of education which takes place in that building during the same fiscal period. Rarely are inflation and the increased costs that develop as a result considered in determining building expenses. As we determined in Chapter 2, our program is diversified and divided into many categorical subsections. However, our format for determining building costs is quite simple. We know exactly how many buildings we have in our system and that number of buildings becomes the subdivisions which we are striving to achieve. Thus, the previous calculations become a firm foundation for developing an actual building cost for each building. Every factor that exists, and every contribution to the educational process which is housed within a building, shares in the total expense of that building. A prerequisite to the building budget concept requires that formulas be developed which accurately ascertain that portion of the total program which should be assigned to each building. These formulas are developed on the basis of students served and educational value rendered by the particular building under construction. These costs may be divided into an unlimited number of categories, including extracurricular functions and subfunctions, and educationally related activities contributing to the total production of the education process.

These program objectives deal with the very basis of the educational process. The functions are derived by incorporating every aspect of the program in which the child participates. Thus, when the picture is complete, all factors are taken into consideration in determining the operating costs incurred by particular buildings throughout the school system. Our task is to identify these costs in the most accurate, concise way possible. Once this is achieved, a firm financial foundation is established, and the stage is set to display the total cost by program of building activities.

To accomplish this accurately, time studies must be carried out. Personnel must be screened, and activities must be analyzed in a way to insure that all time use is accounted for. Assignments must be carefully checked and enrollment must be constantly analyzed. All supporting functions of the school system must be examined thoroughly. The impact of special education upon the building function must be constantly examined. Program objectives with regard to student participation should be incorporated in the total effort of determining the concise nature and related impact of program costs.

Designing Breakdown Formulas

Program costs from Level II which provide other than instructional functions, such as plant maintenance, plant operation, transportation and consultant services, must again be considered on a building basis. These costs may be determined by developing ratios on the basis of square footage and personnel assigned to each building which influence the expense of operating a particular building; the age and physical condition of that building as well as its geographical location (Illus. 3-1). Transportation, of course, may be developed on a pupil ratio basis determined by the actual use. One will usually find these factors are district-wide in nature and applicable to each building on an enrollment ratio scale.

PLANT MAINTENANCE, OPERATION AND TRANSPORTATION

Items Included

50% Supt's Salary
75% Ass't. Supt's Salary
25% Dir. of Inst. Salary
10% Dir. of Child S.C. Salary
100% Trans. Coord. Salary
30% Clerk of Bd. Salary
30% Additional Office Expense

Formula approximation = 40% of line items cost divided on the following basis

15% Plant Maintenance
30% Transportation
55% Plant Operation

Illus. 3-1

Isolation of curricular offerings and cost analysis at Level III varies as to difficulty. As we know, Level II determines programs existing in the school system. However, on Level III many programs do not exist in every grade. For example, industrial arts is not available in grade 1. Therefore, in determining the building costs, it is essential that we consider which programs are available in that building and associate only the costs of those programs with the total cost of operating that particular building. In situations where many buildings are utilized to carry out the function of one program, it is necessary to subdivide those programs in an effort to determine the exact function that each building plays with regard to that factor. Curricular offerings that develop from the junior high or middle school through the senior high school, such as industrial education or career education programs, will require a formula for distribution of costs for each building. These building costs may either be determined by the per pupil expense of students served, or may be developed on the basis of the number of teachers assigned to that program.

When considering the curricular offerings that extend from grade 1 through the senior high program, such as math, science and social studies, we must also develop a formula for the distribution of costs by each building. These formulas on the elementary level may reflect the number of teachers assigned to the buildings expressed in a percentage of the total staff, and at the same time include the percentage of time utilized by each teacher on each subject matter area. This rationale may also be used in developing financial criteria to be used in breaking down the middle school or junior and senior high school programs. It may also be necessary to exclude special education from this division if it is included in another area of the curriculum.

Thus, the determination of an accurate formula for distributing program costs between elementary and junior high programs may be arrived at by determining the number of students served in each program and the number of minutes devoted to each subject area within a particular program. All additional costs will be assigned on a prorated basis, apportioned and determined by the amount of minutes assigned to that program.

Revolutionary Calculations

Any special services of supportive organizations functioning within the building on a Level II basis will be adjusted in terms of teacher units. These programs, and the services provided through the supportive functions, will be construed as being beneficial proportionally to all of the students in a given building. This same rationale can be applied to the expenses of determining library costs, audio-visual costs, and detailed coordination and program administration costs (Illus. 3-2).

CONVERSION FORMULA FOR PLANT OPERATION AND MAINTENANCE COST FOR BOTH JR. HIGH SCHOOL LEVEL II TO LEVEL III

Maintenance-Operation
Formula

Mulberry St. Jr. High

Mathematics	$21 \times 1 = 21$
Language Arts	$35 \times 1 = 35$
Science	$21 \times 1 = 21$
History	$21 \times 1 = 21$
Art	$4 \times 1 = 4$
Music	$4 \times 2 = 8$
Physical Education	$11 \times 4 = 44$
Home Economics	$4 \times 2 = 8$
Industrial Arts	$4 \times 2 = 8$

Illus. 3-2

Learning Resource Center	$6 \times 2 = 12$
Child Study Center	$10 \times 2 = 20$
Student Activities	$2 \times 4 = 8$
Program Administration	$6 \times 1 = \underline{6}$
Total	216

Code:

A. First number represents average periods per day.
B. Second figure is a ratio assigned for building space used.
C. Third figure is used to determine percentage of maintenance and operation cost.
D. Total represents cost of maintenance and operation.

Illus. 3-2 (Con't.)

The cost of maintaining a building involves both the day by day services and the major repairs which are required to maintain the educational program. All of these costs may be developed by the buildings based upon a percentage of the total district-wide building square footage. Other factors which may be included in the formula are aides, condition of buildings, maintenance problems and general building structure.

Any costs which are of an operational nature may also be distributed to each building on a square footage basis. Costs of personnel utilized to maintain the building must also be a part of the formula in order to provide a ratio of production costs. Total personnel costs, including fringe benefits which are applied to a particular building, radically change the cost picture and are forgotten many times in traditional accounting programs (Illus. 3-3)

**CONVERSION FORMULA FOR BOTH JUNIOR HIGH SCHOOLS
PROGRAM ALLOCATIONS OF TRANSPORTATION COSTS
LEVEL II TO LEVEL III**

Mathematics	5
English	5
Social Studies	5
Science	5
Art	1
Music	1
Physical Education	2
Industrial Arts	2
Home Economics	2
Learning Resource Center	1
Child Study Center	.3
Student Activities	.5
Program Administration	.2
Total	30.

Illus. 3-3

A.   The number assigned to each program represents a ratio, based on the number of students involved on a weekly basis.

B.   Total represents the cost of transportation; each program is assigned a percentage of the cost on this formula.

Illus. 3-3 *(Con't.)*

When considering transportation costs, we must remember that although every student is not transported, every student in the district represents, by program, a proportional amount of the transportation expense. For example, a school district which maintains a transportation fleet must distribute the cost of that fleet equally between all system programs and, in turn, on a per pupil basis. If this is not accurately accomplished, then in reality students who are transported assume more than a fair share of the cost which should be attributed to them. Therefore, programs which are used heavily by students who are bussed appear to be more costly than they would be otherwise. It is also important that all field trips, athletic events and other transportation within the school system, not directly related to academic programs, should be prorated according to the program utilization factors. As viewed in Illus. 3-4, all of these calculations should be based upon the best judgment of the administrators responsible for finance and instruction.

CONVERSION FORMULA FOR DIVIDING TOTAL MIDDLE SCHOOL COST BETWEEN THE TWO JR. HIGHS BASED UPON STAFF UTILIZATION FROM LEVEL II TO LEVEL III

A.   The following programs are divided on the basis of enrollment: 6/13 to Pleasant Street and 7/13 to Mulberry Street.

        Art
        Language Arts
        Mathematics
        Science and Health
        Social Studies
        Student Activities
        Child Study Center

B.   The following programs were divided on a 50-50 Basis:

        Learning Resource Center
        Physical Education
        Home Economics
        Industrial Arts
        Music
        Program Administration

Illus. 3-4

Explanations that Sell

Using the rationale that we have established, we can begin a "CAS" analysis. The first calculation to be determined is the apportionment of costs of those programs that involve the middle and senior high school only. These should be developed and established according to the number of teacher units assigned to the high school and two each to the middle schools. If the Level II costs for business education is $80,000, this figure would be divided by the eight teachers to obtain a per teacher unit cost of $10,000. The high school cost would then be $40,000 and $20,000 for each of the two junior highs. As we can see, costs are distributed on a teacher unit basis and the formula developed by dividing the total program cost by the number of teacher units, or by applying the Level II teacher unit percentages applied to the total cost of the program. In this calculation, the teacher unit percentage is the recommended procedure as developed in the Level II formula. The total teacher units may then be assigned to the full or proportional teacher units assigned to each of the elementary, middle schools and high school programs. These units then may be given a mathematical percentage of the total.teaching units existing within the school system.[1]

In a particular school system, the total adjusted teacher units in a district may be 300 units, of which 60% are elementary, 20% middle school and 20% high school. These percentage figures can be applied to each of the total program costs. By applying these percentages, it is possible to determine exactly the portion of total program costs which should be applied to each of the various segments of the school system. Actual building costs then may also be determined by applying the proportional percent of the teachers time to the various elementary and middle schools in the system. The middle school and senior high school costs in turn may be factually established by involving the teacher assigned to each individual building. If, for example, an elementary building has developed a staff which involved 10% of the total elementary teachers, then a language arts program would receive a proportional percentage of the cost contributed to the elementary program. This same procedure may be followed in determining the various percentage of individual program costs for each major division of the school system. By utilizing these established percentages it is possible to determine in every instance the cost of the program in relation to the total cost of building and operation. If more than one senior high or middle school exists within the system, the procedure for determining the costs which apply thereto would be exactly the same as utilized in the elementary program.

---

[1]Mr. Glen Moss, Superintendent of Leetonia Exempted Village Schools, Leetonia, Ohio.

As indicated by Illus. 3-5, in all of the supportable areas which operate within the school system, the same system of cost distribution would be utilized in determining building costs in each of the subject areas. If, for example, the cost of a particular special function within the system was $100,000 and the percentage attached to that function was 50%, then $50,000 would theoretically be the portion of the total program cost which would be applied to that particular function. If a program within a building, for example, uses 35% of the supportive function, then that percentage of total cost would be its share.

CONVERSION FORMULA FROM
LEVEL II TO LEVEL III

Art   Total Unit 11 = $104,871.61

Elem. Unit	Jr. H. Unit	H.S. Unit
6 or .55	3 or .27	2 or .18=
$57,679.39	$28,315.33	$18,876.89

percentage of teachers	$15,007.12	-- MSJH
in each building into	1.6 or .53	
total elem. teachers give		
% of which should be	$13,308.21	-- PSJH
applied to each building	1.4 or .47	

Learning Center   Total Units 3 = $39,859.84

Elem. Unit	Jr. H. Unit	H.S. Unit
1 or .33	1 or .33	1 or .34
$13,153.75	$13,153.75	$13,552.34

Language Arts   Total Units 55 = $840,329.43 (Based on Actual Teachers)

Elem. Unit	Jr. H. Unit	H.S. Unit
35 or .64	10 or .18	10 or .18
$537,810.84	$151,259.30	$151,259.29

Physical Ed.   Total Units 14 = $139,902.53

Elem. Unit	Jr. H. Unit	H.S. Unit
6 or .43	5 or .36	3 or .21
$60,158.09	$50,364.91	$29,379.53

Home Economics   Total Units 4 = $48,724.73 (Based on Actual Teachers)

Jr. H. Unit	H.S. Unit
$24,362.36	$24,362.37

Industrial Arts   Total Units 4 = $49,350.03 (Based on Actual Units)

Jr. H. Unit	H.S. Unit
$24,525.01	$24,525.02

Illus. 3-5

Math   Total Units 25 = $286,672.49

Elem. Unit	Jr. H. Unit	H.S. Unit
11 or .44	6 or .24	8 or .32
$126,135.90	$68,801.40	$91,735.19

Music   Total Units = Same as Art = $100,840.15

Elem. Unit	Jr. H. Unit	H.S. Unit
.55	.27	.18
$55,462.08	$27,226.84	$18,151.23

Science &   Total Units 20 = $258,051.73
Health

Elem. Unit	Jr. H. Unit	H.S. Unit
7 or .35	5 or .25	8 or .40
$90,318.11	$64,512.93	$103,220.69

Plant Main-   Total Units = $57,606.46
tenance

Plant   Total Units = $413,365.02
Operation

Washington	=	.038
Central	=	.023
Columbia	=	.044
Lincoln	=	.038
East	=	.038
Oak	=	.035
Maple	=	.027
North	=	.021
West	=	.033
South	=	.043
Pine	=	.172
Hancock	=	.116
Sr. High	=	.372

Social   Total Units 19 = $253,966.85
Studies

Elem. Unit	Jr. H. Unit	H.S. Unit
7 or .37	6 or .31	6 or .32
$93,967.73	$78,729.72	$81,269.40

Illus. 3-5 *(Con't.)*

Student   Total Units 4 = $42,479.77
Activities

Elem. Unit	Jr. H. Unit	H.S. Unit
.25	.25	.50
$10,619.94	$10,619.94	$21,239.89

Program   Total Units 10 = $194,872.20
Admin.

Elem. Unit	Jr. H. Unit	H.S. Unit
6 or .60	2 or .20	2 or .20
$116,923.32	$38,974.44	$38,974.44

Child   Total Units 12 = $199,939.33
Study
Center

Elem. Unit	Jr. H. Unit	H.S. Unit
7 or .59	2 or .17	3 or .24
$117,964.20	$33,989.69	$47,985.44

Transpor-   Based Upon 3300 Students Being Transported
tation
               $129,521.72/3300   Unit cost $39.25 per student per year

Kinder- $73,073.75   7.5=7= $9,743.17
garten   ½ 4,871.56

Illus. 3-5 *(Con't.)*

Using this rationale, but applying it in a different way, finds all of the maintenance and operation costs being divided on a percentage of the total square feet of building space in each district. If, for example, a building has 10% of the total square feet available and the total percentage of the maintenance equals $64,000, then the maintenance costs would be $6,400. If this is an older building or in need of repair, a portion of the total percentage of maintenance should be added as a correction factor. Thus, the result is a weighted proportion of the total maintenance area, as interpreted in square feet and calculated on a percentage of the total cost involved.

This same formula may be used to distribute operational costs throughout the system. Once again any building needing repair, recently repaired, or in need of additions should be adjusted so that the weighted factor will contribute to a more realistic figure.

All transportation costs may be prorated per the actual building enrollment. If these costs exceed the district total, then the calcuations must be adjusted. For example, if the annual transportation cost for the district totaled $130,000 and the district has 5,000 pupils, the cost per pupil annually would equal $26.00. This multiplied by the buildings enrollment would equal the buildings share of the transportation costs.

The establishment of such costs is essential in determining the total calculations for the building involved. In order to insure validity within the process, it is necessary to prove each program column before those costs are moved on as a part of the total calculation. Reevaluation of the calculation may be required, and must be completed accurately before proceeding on to the next phase of calculation. When all of these figures are found to be accurate and form a mathematical picture of the district's program priorities, then we are ready to begin applying these calculations to the various buildings within the system.

The formulas used in developing Level III of the CAS system should be reviewed and reevaluated on a semiannual basis. Once changes in the total mix of the formula have been identified, these calculations should be adjusted to reflect the constant changing building program allocation relationship. The final calculations should be established for future reference, and revisions should be made as needs develop for more accurate financial designations. As you rework these formulas, you will find less and less dependence on accurate estimates, and more on actual figures as you gather more data related to a CAS system.

In many school systems, these calculations will be the first attempt to break down segments of the curriculum into cost factors by program. As a result, misinterpretation may develop. In order to compensate for such an eventuality, a detailed program of staff in-service must be followed. Calculations should be presented in easy to understand, highly simplified format, punctuated by brief, concise explanations as Illus. 3-6 exhibits. Experienced educators and administrators within the system who have developed CAS should be involved in the dissemination of the information gained from the process. Every effort should be made to provide detailed explanations and concise, factual examples of the calculations being performed. The entire team of administrators should work together to develop a concise format, regulated by consistency with regard to disseminating the detailed information.

Public Relations and Results

In general, however, you will start with a plus, since the Board of Education, staff and students will be interested in this method of determining costs, and the professional staff is equipped to understand the detailed explanations provided. Lay factions of the community will also be in-

PROPORTIONAL PERCENT OF GRADE 1-5 ELEMENTARY
TEACHER TIME ASSIGNED BY BUILDING TO EACH PROGRAM

Level III

Building Code	Elementary Bldg.	Teachers	Percent
50	North	7	10
51	Central	6	8.6
52	Columbia	10	14.3
53	Roosevelt	10	14.3
54	East	10	14.3
55	South	10	14.3
56	Washington	7	10
57	Lincoln	4	5.6
58	West[2]	6	8.6

Illus. 3-6

terested in the cost breakdown as it relates to the practical development of an efficient system of financial spending.

The greatest value of the Cost Analysis System relates to the Board of Education and their function as the accountable officials of the community. CAS provides a basis for factual solutions to long ignored problems of financial allocations. Boards of Education may use these calculations in developing well coordinated financial documents to be disseminated throughout the community. This information becomes invaluable in convincing the community that financial needs exist within the school system. All of these factors contribute to orderly campaigns for additional levy funds and renewed operating funds. Other educational institutions within the general area become interested in the financial calculations developed within the school system. As a result, the school system develops prestige within the total educational community. This prestige is transfered to the administration and Board of Education, which have calculated and organized the financial system. In even the most simple form, the program analysis of the cost by building is a great improvement over former methods of reporting functional costs within the school system. Although this system is independent in and of itself as part of the total CAS procedure, Level III becomes a valuable input into the final calculations, which must be available to determine an effective appropriation and budgeting document.

---

[2]Does not include special education.

A constant and real danger of Level III is the development of dependence upon the variables which can distort calculations and misrepresent a financial priority.

Every effort should be made to design the most effective procedure available to gain valid information needed to determine the financial facts which are required within the system.

Once completed, Level III becomes a base for the development of the remainder of the CAS system. In order to proceed, additional information, personnel involvement and equipment is needed. Level II program costs, as well as Level II adjusted teacher units, must be available in order to move into Level III of the CAS system. As we move from Level III to Level IV of our program, a listing of teachers by elementary, middle school and senior high school levels is required. Also, a listing of all employees by subject matter and assignment will be needed in order to analyze their physical role. A complete and concise analysis of student enrollment by building and grade level will be required in Level IV calculations.

In general, the central office personnel and the fiscal officer will be involved in the final calculations. As in proceeding functions within the system, calculators and analysis instruments must be made available to the committee responsible for developing the CAS system.

Once Level III is completed, the system will have available a complete set of financial documents based upon the cost as interpreted through building programs within the system. This information will become a valuable asset in determining the future financial priorities within the school system.

Elements Needed for Success

The following information is needed in order to be prepared to move into the next levels of operation. Illus. 3-7, 3-8 and 3-9 provide examples of the essential information.

A COMPLETE LISTING OF INSTRUCTIONAL PROGRAMS AND DESCRIPTIONS

Code No.

05   *Language Arts*—This figure includes the total of our elementary English, writing, reading and spelling programs, plus all secondary English and reading programs (our total Language Arts Program) which includes a percentage of the cost of the following line items: Administration, Instructional, Coordinate Activities, Libraries, Transportation of Pupils, Auxiliary Agencies, Operation of the School Plant, Maintenance of the School Plant and Capital Outlay. We receive a total of $1250

Illus. 3-7

from NDEA Title III, which helps to finance this particular program. Fifty percent (50%) of each elementary teacher's time is also charged to the cost of this program.

06   *Foreign Language*—This figure includes the total cost of our present Foreign Language Program, which includes a percentage of the cost of the following line items: Administration, Instructional, Coordinate Activities, Libraries, Transportation of Pupils, Auxiliary Agencies, Operation of the School Plant, Maintenance of the School Plant and Capital Outlay. We receive a total of $625 from the NDEA Title III, which helps to finance this particular program.

08   *Physical Education*—This figure includes the total cost of our present Physical Education Program, which includes a percentage of the cost of the following line items: Administration, Instructional, Coordinate Activities, Libraries, Transportation of Pupils, Auxiliary Agencies, Operation of the School Plant, Maintenance of the School Plant, Recreational Activities, and Capital Outlay. Five percent (5%) of each elementary teacher's time is charged to this program.

09   *Home Economics*—This figure includes the total cost of our Home Economics Program, which includes a percentage of the cost of the following line items: Administration, Instructional, Coordinate Activities, Libraries, Transportation of Pupils, Auxiliary Agencies, Operation of the School Plant, Maintenance of the School Plant and Capital Outlay. Approximately $1200 federal funds are divided on a proportional basis between Vocational Home Economics, B.O.E., and Vocational Agriculture each year. It might be noted that this amount will be likely to decrease in the coming year.

10   *Industrial Arts*—This figure includes the total cost of our Industrial Arts Program, which includes a percentage of the cost of all the line items listed under learning resource centers. We receive a total of $625 from NDEA Title III, which helps to finance this particular program.

11   *Mathematics*—This figure includes the total cost of our Mathematics Program, which includes a percentage of the cost of all the line items listed under learning resource centers. We receive a total of $625 from NDEA Title III, which helps to finance this particular program. Fifteen percent (15%) of each elementary teacher's time is charged to this program.

Illus. 3-7 *(Con't.)*

CONVERSION FORMULA FOR CALCULATING BUILDING COST FROM PROGRAM COST CALCULATIONS

			Enrollment
Elementary	.52	K-6	568
Junior High	.16	7-8	176
Senior High	.32	9-12	349

Illus. 3-8

A CODED LISTING OF ALL BUILDINGS WITHIN THE SCHOOL SYSTEM

LEVEL III–BUILDING

50	North	Elementary School
51	Central	Elementary School
52	Columbia	Elementary School
53	Washington	Elementary School
54	East	Elemetnary School
55	South	Elementary School
56	Roosevelt	Elementary School
57	Lincoln	Elementary School
58	West	Elementary School
59	Hickory	Middle School
60	Maple	Middle School
61	Senior	High School

Illus. 3-9

4

Generating Public Appeal for Grade Level Costs

Introduction to Grade Level Cost Concepts

All school systems developing a programming approach to spending should have a breakdown of their current budget by grade levels. The advantages to the grade level breakdown include a comparative knowledge of each grade level, K-8, within the school system. A grade level break-down is not conducive to the secondary program which involves specialized subject matter divided into departments. For this reason, as we develop a grade level breakdown of our spending program, we will concentrate our efforts on grades Kindergarten through Eight or Nine, according to the progressive arrangement of the various grade levels by building within your system. This concept of fiscal accountability is unique because seldom do school systems have a reference as to the exact cost of any particular grade level within the system. This information is valuable in comparing the progressive increases in cost as one moves from grade one to grade three within the system. After we have discussed how one arrives at an accurate grade level approximation, we will consider the differences which one finds between various grade levels and the explanation which may be attached to these differences. For example, you might discover that grade one is three or four thousand dollars more or less expensive than grade two. If this is true, how can you determine the exact cause of this difference in cost? These and other similar questions must be answered before one can completely understand the rationale behind current spending policies within the school district. These are usually unpopular questions among school administrators merely because they are difficult questions to answer. The cost accountability system that we are considering provides us with the essential tools to answer questions such as why different grade levels cost different amounts of money, and why these vary from year to year as a result of changes in personnel and enrollment.

The Benefit of the Grade Level Cost Concept

Notice Illus. 4-1, entitled "Anytown's Cost Accountability Elementary Level Listing of the Projected Appropriations." Notice that each grade level has been broken down according to the subject matter which is covered by that grade level. For example, at the first grade level, we have the total of fifteen hundred minutes per week. This time is divided into groupings for each subject matter area covered during the first grade. All of these figures are contained in the State of Ohio's Minimum Standards for Elementary Programs. By establishing the cost at the first grade level, it is easy to see how we can move to a subject matter breakdown of cost appropriations.

How do we arrive at the cost, which we show in Illus. 4-1 as $287,938.18, as the exact cost of operating the first grade within our school system? What facts do we know about our current spending which can help us determine the exact cost of any particular grade level? We all certainly know by this time how much it costs to operate a given building within the system. Thus, the building cost becomes the key for the foundation to developing an accurate, accountable breakdown of grade level appropriations. We simply establish from Level II the cost of operating each building within the system. By using this established, fixed cost, we then determine the appropriate percentage represented by each grade level within that building.

ANYTOWN'S COST ACCOUNTABILITY
ELEMENTARY LEVEL LISTING
OF THE 19-- PROJECTED APPROPRIATIONS

KINDERGARTEN:

The Mount Vernon School District Kindergarten Program for the 19-- Fiscal year will be held during two and one-half hour sessions. Kindergarten provides students with an introduction to the curriculum areas of reading, health and safety, social studies and mathematics.

The cost of this program is $99,096.99, ninety per cent (90%) which is state supported and ten per cent (10%), or $9,909.69, from local taxes.

ELEMENTARY:

Average Minutes Per Week

Grade	1st	2nd	3rd	4th, 5th
Opening Exercises	50	50	50	75
Reading	600	600	450	300
Language Development	150	---	---	---
Language	---	250	350	225
Handwriting	100	---	---	---
Mathematics	150	150	150	200
Social Studies	90	90	120	200
Science and Health	60	60	80	200
Art	60	55	60	80

Illus. 4-1

Music	60	60	70	80
Physical Education	30	60	70	80
Recess	150	125	100	60
TOTAL	1500	1500	1500	1500

PROJECTED	$287,938.18		$298,864.15	4th $261,127.82
APPROPRIATIONS		$303,766.22		5th $308,683.19

The above figures include the total projected costs of operating the described programs as outlined. These figures include every cost associated with the operations of these programs.

Illus. 4-1 *(Con't.)*

ANYTOWN'S COST ACCOUNTABILITY
MIDDLE SCHOOL LISTING
OF THE 19-- PROJECTED APPROPRIATIONS

Boys and girls in early adolescence face many new, emotional, physical, intellectual, social, and moral problems. We believe the middle school organization should create an atmosphere in which each youth can be helped to recognize his strengths and weaknesses, grow in self understanding, and be encouraged to express himself in the light of these understandings so that his best efforts are displayed as an individual and as a member of our society.

THE MIDDLE SCHOOL PROGRAM:

The Middle School Program for the 19-- Fiscal year will include directed instruction in the areas listed below:

Sixth Grade: (Self-contained classrooms), Projected Cost: $265,286.39

English	Science-Health	Music
Reading	Social Studies	Physical Education
Spelling	Art	

Seventh Grade: (Block-time classes), Projected Cost: $255,686.31

Language Arts-Social Studies	Industrial Arts
Mathematics-Science and Health	Home Economics
Art	Physical Education
Music	

Eighth Grade: (Departmentalized classes), Projected Cost: $259,791.86

Language Arts	Mathematics	Art
American History	Industrial Arts	Music
Science-Health	Home Economics	Physical Education

On a voluntary basis, students will have the opportunity to participate in special music groups at each grade level. Intramural sports will be available for boys and girls interested, and there will be an interscholastic sports program available to boys in grades seven and eight.

Illus. 4-2

The Crosswalk Concept in Illus. 4-3 shows us the method by which the breakdown to grade levels is achieved. Notice that Oak School has a budget of $500.00 divided by five grades possessing one teacher each, or at a budget figure of $100.00 per grade. Although this is an overly simplified explanation of grade level achievement, it does provide us with the general concept. In more complicated situations, it will be necessary to assign a percentage to each grade level, representing the percentage of total staff time utilized by that grade level in order to achieve the objectives of the current instructional program. Once this percentage has been identified and rationalized, it becomes the representative percentage which will be applied to the total cost of operating that particular school building. For example, if the first grade should represent 12 percent of the total $500 allocation to Oak School, as viewed in Illus. 4-1, then the 12 percent figure would also apply to the $500 in order to determine the cost of grade one in Oak School. Thus by developing a percentage ratio based upon the actual amount of time utilized by each professional staff member within a building, it is possible to determine the exact cost of operating any particular grade within any particular building within the system.

"CROSSWALK CONCEPT" LEVEL III
BUILDING BREAKDOWN TO LEVEL IV
GRADE LEVEL BREAKDOWN

	Building		
Grade Level	Oak	Pine	Maple
Grade 1	$100		
Grade 2	100		
Grade 3	100		
Grade 4	100		
Grade 5	100		
TOTAL	$500		

Illus. 4-3

Forceful Breakdown Formulas

Let us now turn our attention to the differences between grade level cost, specifically Kindergarten through eighth grade within a school system. We notice in Illus. 4-1 that it costs a little over $300,000 to operate the second grade. However, as we look at the seventh grade, we notice it costs $255,000. What could be the possible differences in these two cost figures? Remember, it is necessary to take into consideration not only the amount of professional staff time involved in carrying out a program called the seventh grade, but also the number of students involved in that particular program, and the amount of equipment and building space which is utilized in order to actualize the program. All of these factors become important ingredients in determining the overall cost of operating that program. Remember, a projected cost accountability system represents a time study of all of the personnel involved in the completion of a particular academic program within a school system. Time is the factor we are measuring. We are measuring time in terms of its monetary value, as it is a measure of the spending pattern within our school system. Time represents money, and wasted time represents wasted money. Therefore, as we develop our cost accountability system, we must be constantly cognizant of the value of each minute of each professional's time, and how that individual applies his day to accomplishing the goals of the current instructional program. Wasted effort in terms of small pupil-teacher ratio, or in terms of small pupil-building ratio, can represent a loss in valuable dollars and a loss of credibility to taxpayers within the system. As conscientious administrators, it is our duty and our responsibility to provide the most possible educational value for each tax dollar spent on instructional program within our school district. To this end, we can be held accountable for the effect our spending patterns have on the educational progress of the students within our school district. An accurate grade level breakdown can provide these facts, and improve our credibility within the community.

Creative Calculations

The utilization potential of a grade level cost breakdown is unlimited. For example, in Illus. 4-4, we consider exactly how a building breakdown is achieved on the basis of staff and the percentage of staff represented. Illus. 4-4 shows us that we had a total of 70 teachers in all of our elementary buildings. By dividing the number of teachers in any given building into the total number of teachers, a percentage is achieved which represents that building. For example, 7 teachers divided by 70 equals 10 percent. These percentage figures represent then the amount of finances utilized within that particular building. Of course, it is necessary that all of the elementary building's percentages equal 100 percent. In some cases, however, you might arrive at a distorted approximation because of one of the following facts:

1. A building could contain many first year teachers, very low on the salary schedule, and thus the overall effect would be a low approximation of the cost of operating that building.

2. More importantly, a building might have an experienced staff which places all teachers very high on the salary schedule, and thus the percentage of teachers would provide a cost approximation which would be less than the approximation which should be assigned to that building.

Therefore, it could be possible that a weighting formula would need to be devised. This situation exists when a building has a very small number of staff members and all of them find themselves at one or other extreme of the salary schedule. For this reason, it is important, when determining cost breakdowns within a building, that one must consider the position on the salary schedule each teacher finds himself. If it is necessary to weight a particular building in the system, then always move the percentage used for the weighting process from the largest building involving the largest number of teachers and the largest number of funds, to the smaller buildings involving the smaller number of teachers and smaller amounts of funds. By following this general rule of thumb, it is possible to arrive at accurate approximations within 5 percent of the true value or cost of that given program. Remember, weighting is usually not necessary. It should only be used in extreme cases where the teacher population within a given building is not representative of the total population of the system. In these cases, it is essential that a weighting formula be devised which will best represent the true cost of operating a given program within a given building.

PROPORTIONAL PERCENT OF GRADE 1-5 ELEMENTARY TEACHER TIME ASSIGNED BY BUILDING TO EACH PROGRAM BASED UPON STATE MINIMUM STANDARDS

Level III

Building Code	Elementary Bldg.	Teachers	Percent
50	North	7	10
51	Central	6	8.6
52	Columbia	10	14.3
53	Washington	10	14.3
54	East	10	14.3
55	Roosevelt	10	14.3
56	South	7	10
57	Pine	4	5.6
58	West[1]	6	8.6
		70	100%

Illus. 4-4

---

[1]Does not include special education

Instructions and Explanations

Different weighting formulas may be devised according to individual's actual income as listed on the payroll, or numbers of teachers actually teaching within the building, or an average of incomes within a given building times the number of teachers within that building. The important fact is to use a weighting formula which best represents the solution for the purpose for which the weighting formula has been devised. If this policy is followed, then the results of the weighting process will be accurate and, in turn, the approximations of cost for that particular building will be accurate. If this is accomplished, the accuracy of the total system improves and the cost accountability system becomes a reality.

Another factor which should be considered a grade level cost breakdown is transportation. Illus. 4-5 represents one method of determining a transportation cost breakdown of a particular school system. Notice that in Illus. 4-5, an average cost per student per year for transportation is used. This figure is arrived at by dividing the total number of students in the school district utilizing the transportation by the total cost of the transportation program. This, of course, provides an average cost per student for the service. By multiplying the average per pupil cost of transportation by the number of students in a given building, one determines the amount that transportation costs for a given building within the school system. There are many ramifications to this concept of cost analysis. For example, one might determine a percentage of the total transportation cost by dividing out the percentage of students utilizing transportation within a given building. If this method is used and best represents the number of students utilizing the transportation facilities within the school system, then its use is justified. However, if an average transportation cost per student best represents the apportionment of the total expense of transportation, then the average cost should be used. In general, only students actually using transportation should be counted for a particular building's portion of the total cost of the transportation program. However, in some cases where buildings are located in difficult geographic locations, it might be necessary to weight the expense of transporting students to one building which is located in the far corner of a school district, where, on the other hand, a more centrally located building might represent less cost in terms of transporting students. Weighting transportation is a simple matter. One must only determine the average cost per student, approximate the difference between the applicable percentage in any given building and the acutal cost of transportation for that building, and weight the actual figure by the number of students represented by the difference. Once again, the weighting process is an exception, rather than a general rule, because in most school systems the buildings are generally centralized in location to best represent the student body of the school system. Only in extreme cases, where a school system does not have a sufficient number of buildings to accommodate the population at a given grade level, will it be necessary to utilize a weighting formula for the purpose of determing exact transportation costs. These transportation costs become one more factor in determining an accurate appraisal of the expense involved in operating one building which is a part of the total school system. An effort should always be made to determine the most accurate component of a given system in order to provide the most accurate appraisal of the total cost of operating that particular building. In some cases, weighting is essential, in others, weighting is just an additional guarantee that the final result will fall within a 5 percent approximation of the actual cash expenditure. As one moves into an accountability system, we must realize that year after year, the cost approximations become more accurate, and the 5 percent error factor can be reduced to 3, 2 or even 1 percent, thus giving a credible, accurate accounting of the system's expenditures for any given building, grade level or subject within the instructional program. All of these factors must be considered when developing the total concept of the accountability system. Transportation alone represents only one component. However, the accuracy of developing these figures is only represented in the accuracy of the total project.

TRANSPORTATION CONVERSION FORMULA FOR
LEVEL III EXPENDITURE BREAKDOWN

Level III Code	School	No. of Students	Cost
50	North	234	$ 9,184.50
51	Central	30	1,177.50
52	Columbia	235	9,223.75
53	Washington	55	2,158.75
54	East	100	3,925.00
55	South	160	6,280.00
56	Roosevelt	230	9,027.50
57	Pine	60	2,355.00
58	West	70	2,747.50

Illus. 4-5

59	North East J.H.	430	16,877.50
60	South West J.H.	340	13,341.72
61	Sr. High School	1356	53,223.00
		3300	$129,521.72

Cost per student per year = $39.25

Note: The total of 3300 students including all field trips and other misc. transportation provided pupils by the school district.

Illus. 4-5 *(Con't.)*

Exciting Results

Remember that the object of a grade level breakdown is to establish a foundation on Level IV of our accountability system for entry into Level V of our system. This means that the final result of our Level IV breakdown should be a concise analysis of spending at each grade level. In order to accomplish this at the grade levels which constitute the junior high school program or the middle school program, we should consider the example given in Illus. 4-6. Here we view a breakdown of all courses offered at the middle school level: Art, learning centers, language arts, physical education and all of the other courses which make up the middle school or junior high program. These courses must be broken down in terms of the percentage of each grade level within that building that that course represents. For example, consider the Art Program at the middle school listed in Illus. 4-6. Thirty percent of that program is apportioned to grade level six, 30 percent to grade level seven and 40 percent to grade level eight. This could mean that there is one art teacher within the building, and that teacher's time has been divided proportionately over the three grade levels. If we look at the explanation of Illus. 4-6 under the subject matter area of Home Economics, we find that no part of the Home Economics Program has been apportioned to the sixth grade. This is because Home Economics is only offered in grades seven and eight, and because the teacher's time has been equally divided between seven and eight. This is evidence that an equal number of seventh and eighth grade students are served by the teacher. This concept, or approach, to subject apportionment to grade levels is a common method of determining the percentage of cost which should be applied to a particular grade level within a building. As we move further in Level V, or subject matter breakdown of cost, we realize that Level IV is essential to determining exact cost approximation for grade level spending.

CONVERSION FORMULA FOR JR. HIGH SCHOOL PROGRAMS
BASED UPON TIME UTILIZATION FROM
LEVEL III TO LEVEL IV[2]

	Grade 6	Grade 7	Grade 8	
Art	30	30	40	= 100%
Learning Center	30	35	35	
Language Arts	60	20	20	
Physical Education	20	40	40	
Home Economics	0	50	50	
Industrial Arts	0	50	50	
Math	30	35	35	
Music	40	30	30	
Science & Health	30	35	35	
Social Studies	30	35	35	
Student Activities	20	40	40	
Program Administration	33	33	34	
Child study Center	33	33	34	

Illus. 4-6

These figures, although they represent an approximation of spending, also become the following year's appropriation foundation. A school administrator can easily determine his appropriation document from last year's budget. By altering the appropriation document, and changing the various program emphasis through allocating more funds for one subject matter area and less funds for another subject matter area, last year's budget becomes next year's appropriations. The accountability system approach to appropriations allows a more exact apportionment of funds designed to serve the instructional program and academic subject matter concentration. A school administrator aware of the ramifications of poor fiscal allocations can easily rectify his approach by utilizing to the ultimate extreme all of the facts which are available with an accountability based system. Notice the concentration and analysis which must be an integral part of the development of a concise accountability cost breakdown in order to achieve accuracy within the estimations. Notice that each category of the curriculum must be covered and must be analyzed in order to include all cost factors which represent the program of instruction in the final fiscal allocations. When the time comes to determine new appropriation documents, these factors and those figures will become the base, or the foundation, for the determination of a concise budgetary allocation

---

[2]Figures represent percentage allocation to each grade level based on time factor.

within the fiscal potential of the school system. The limitations imposed by the various grade level appropriations will intensify the overall fiscal credibility of the school system utilizing this approach to spending. In order to determine the true accuracy of the appropriation document and later the budgetary instrument, it is essential that checks and balances, cross-checks and cross analysis be utilized by the administrative team. They should be utilized in the effort to increase efficiency with regard to fiscal spending, and to increase credibility among the tax paying public, which supports the school system and, in the end analysis, finances the total instructional program. A cost accountability system can provide fiscal credibility within the system.

The purpose of our cost accountability system is to reduce cost within the school system and to make more efficient the total fiscal spending within the school system. The following are some of the possible methods of utilizing some of this information at this level.

The elimination of non-teaching uses of teacher time that reduce the number of classes which teachers can handle is one possible use. Instructional salaries will go down, thus saving additional funds. Also, new teachers can be hired that are younger and have less experience, thus are lower paid personnel and can be used for non-teaching tasks.

The use of paraprofessionals, under teacher supervision whenever possible, is an alternative. The school system will spend less money for higher paid professional jobs. Of course, there will be howls from the teacher's union and association for hiring the lower paid paraprofessionals for the district.

It may be necessary to reduce the number of very small classes, especially in the high school. This will cause instructional salaries to go down. Also, there will be fewer curricular choices for students and less individualized attention for them.

It is possible to replace credentialed educators in administrative positions with individuals having a business or financial background. In some states, this would require a waiver of certification. This will result in administrative costs going down in systems where you have been paying chiefly for credentials. However, at the same time, communication problems between educators and businessmen might arise.

It is possible that you might want to reduce unplanned variations in class sizes by taking the least desirable pupil-teacher ratio you now have and making it standard for your district. In this case, instructional salaries will go down. However, class size will increase in some of your buildings.

You might determine that you need to increase the number of years between new book adoptions, or revise your fee schedule for students and increase replacement costs to students who deface books. In this case, your book costs will go down. However, teaching materials not always current could force opposition from students, parents and teachers and, in the end analysis, cause teachers to utilize other means of providing educational materials at equally high costs.

In most school systems, it would be possible to charge fees and tuition sufficent to cover the costs of all community education and services. The result of this would be community education costs will go down. However, the decreased use of school might generate much community opposition.

It is possible that the school system might wish to place all or some curriculum development on a contractual basis, or adapt curriculums which are similar to other districts instead of developing a district's own approach. This, of course, will reduce general developmental costs. However, a less tailored approach to your own district's needs, payment of fees, and the poor development of bias curriculums would certainly mean poor communication within the school system, and less effective instructional programs.

Building design is another area where one may cut costs. For example, standard building designs might be utilized instead of custom building designs. This utilization will, of course, reduce the cost of architectural services, and some construction costs may go down. However, these buildings will be less flexible and will not provide an atmosphere for innovation within the facilities. The use of existing facilities on a twelve month basis or on a twelve hour day can also reduce costs. This would provide for capital and allow per pupil plant operations expenses to go down. However, there could be staff and community opposition to the utilization of facilities on a time schedule such as this. Sometimes there are difficulties in arranging contractual agreements, and, in the last analysis, buildings still deteriorate according to the amount of time they are used. Therefore, maintenance and upkeep increases along with cost for housing increases.

Review of the district-wide inventory levels on an annual basis, midway through the school year, will cause the inventory balance and distribution of goods to improve, and inventory costs will go down. The result of this will be increased fiscal credibility within the school system.

Conscientious administrators can tighten up protection and physical control of materials and supplies. As a result of this, losses will be reduced and costs will go down. This procedure is usually well accepted among the community.

As you can see, the above information and concepts can provide a base for an organized, responsible approach to fiscal accountability. This approach is much needed in public schools, and can help develop credibility for administrators and school boards in the execution of their diverse responsibilities. An accurate, grade level breakdown of spending within the school system is essential to the development of this credibility. Without an accurate and complete fiscal foundation, it is impossible for the conscientious school administrator to itemize the essential cost represented by a given instructional program. These costs represent his imagination and the Board's planning in terms of the development of the instructional process. Without fully utilizing the specialities available to him within the instructional staff, and without requiring administrative responsibility with regard to fiscal spending, it is impossible for the conscentious head administrator to determine an accurate course for the fiscal development of his school system. Taking these factors into consideration, what are the essentials for the further development of a cost accountability system?

At this point in the development of your program, all teachers within the school system must be indoctrinated with regard to the purpose and potential of the cost accountability process. All building level administrators must have a thorough knowledge of the internal fiscal workings of the school system, development of appropriation documents, and budgets. They must be involved in the control of inventories and the development of instructional programs. Together the staff, the students, the community and the Board of Education must strive to develop a well organized, planned approach to the instructional objectives as determined by the philosophy of the school system. Both certified and classified personnel must be involved in determining spending policies for the development of appropriation documents. Priorities must be set with regard to every phase of the school program. The system must move toward an objective, responsible spending procedure through the utilization of the talents of all the personnel, students and public within the system. All resources available must be utilized and a coordinated effort is necessary to develop the most practical and the most efficient system possible for spending the taxpayers money, and for accounting for the dollars spent in the instructional process.

When all the above has been accomplished, and a timetable established for further development of the program, then the system is prepared to progress into the subject matter breakdown of fiscal costs within the system. Without the above foundation, a subject matter breakdown of fiscal expenditures is usually questioned because it lacks the integrity of the specialization available within the school district and, thus, lacks credibility.

In order to accomplish the above, mass orientation sessions, as well as small group instruction, must be utilized. Outside experts should be brought into the system. And individual projects should be assigned to various groups within the system. All in all, total mobilization of staff, students, parents and community leaders is essential.

Items and Information Needed to Succeed

The following illustrations present in an orderly format the information which is needed to successfully begin Level V "CAS" calculations.

"CAS" ANALYSIS OF TEACHER USE
BREAKDOWN IN MINUTES FOR ONE SCHOOL DISTRICT

	Senior High	Junior High	Later Elementary	Early Elementary	Average Time	Percent of Time
Total teacher hours	480	450	435	435	450	100%
Actual Classroom time	330	273	309	272	296	65.8
Preparation time	80	102	86	123	98	21.7
Passing time	40	45	10	10	26	5.8
Lunch time	30	30	30	30	30	6.7

Illus. 4-7

CONVERSION FORMULA FOR DIVIDING TOTAL MIDDLE
SCHOOL COST BETWEEN TWO JR. HIGHS BASED
UPON STAFF UTILIZATION FROM LEVEL II TO LEVEL III

A. The following programs were divided on the basis of enrollment: 6/13 to South Jr. High and 7/13 to North Jr. High.

    Art
    Language Arts
    Mathematics
    Science & Health
    Social Studies
    Student Activities
    Child Study Center

B. The following programs were divided on a 50-50 basis:

    Learning Resource Center
    Physical Education
    Home Economics
    Industrial Arts
    Music
    Program Administration

Illus. 4-8

A COMPLETE CODED LISTING OF ALL GRADE LEVEL DIVISIONS WITHIN THE SCHOOL DISTRICT[3]

LEVEL IV–GRADE LEVEL

00	Kindergarten
01	First Grade
02	Second Grade
03	Third Grade
04	Fourth Grade
05	Fifth Grade
06	Sixth Grade
07	Seventh Grade
08	Eighth Grade
09	Ninth Grade
10	Tenth Grade
11	Eleventh Grade
12	Twelfth Grade

Illus. 4-9

LEVEL III TO LEVEL IV PERCENTAGE AND ENROLLMENT STATISTICS[4]

Grade	Percentage	Students
K	.146	83
1	.132	75
2	.142	81
3	.156	89
4	.150	85
5	.134	76
6	.140	79
	1.000	568
7	.494	87
8	.506	89
	1.000	176
9	.300	105
10	.260	91
11	.203	70
12	.237	83
	1.000	349

Illus. 4-10

[3]This list could include areas such as special and vocational education if they are to appear separately and not as part of individual grade levels.

[4]This illustration exhibits a typical percentage and enrollment pattern which might be representative of an average school district. It is impossible to proceed to Level IV without the above statistics concerning your district.

A COST BREAKDOWN OF
GRADE 9
IN A TYPICAL DISTRICT

TOTAL COST

English 9	$13,875.98
Practical Science	9,284.67
General Science	9,284.67
Algebra I	9,284.67
General Math	9,284.67
9th Girls Health & P.E.	9,284.67
Woodworking - Ind. Arts	9,284.67
9th Boys Health & P.E.	9,284.67
General Business	4,693.35
Spanish I	4,693.35
Home Ec. I	4,591.32
Art I	4,591.32
Latin I	4,591.32

PER PUPIL COST

Latin I	$459.13
Woodworking - Ind. Arts	371.38
Home Ec. I	306.08
General Science	273.07
Algebra I	257.90
Art I	241.64
Practical Science	232.11
9th Girls Health & P.E.	197.54
Spanish I	195.55
9th Boys Health & P.E.	185.69
English 9	182.57
General Math	182.05
General Business	151.39

Above is a total cost and per pupil cost breakdown of a typical school district. Each grade level should be calculated in the above manner.

Illus. 4-11

A COST BREAKDOWN OF TYPICAL
VOCATIONAL PROGRAMS
INDEPENDENT OF GRADE LEVELS

TOTAL COST

Cosmetology I (International School of Cosmetology)	$750.00
D.C.T. Diversified Co-op Training	203.00
C.O.E. Co-op Office Experience	199.96
O.W.E. Occupational Work Experience	173.28
Child Care	139.67
Graphic Arts	124.99
D.C.T. Diversified Co-op Training	119.90
Production Agriculture	93.18

PER PUPIL COST

D.C.T. Diversified Co-op Training	$203.00
O.W.E. Occupational Work Experience	173.28
Child Care	139.67
Cosmetology I (International School of Cosmetology)	125.00
Graphic Arts	124.99
D.C.T. Diversified Co-op Training	119.90
C.O.E. Co-op Office Experience	99.98
Production Agriculture	93.18

The above figures represent the exact cost allocation for a typical vocational program which is not a part of your normal grade level structure. These courses might be housed in a joint vocational school or by means of a vocational cooperative district. They could also be part of your normal high school curriculum.

Illus. 4-12

A COST BREAKDOWN OF STUDY HALLS

TOTAL COST

Study Hall (155)	$3,345.21
Study Hall (301)	3,345.21
Study Hall (178)	3,345.21
Study Hall (178)	3,345.21
Study Hall (178)	3,345.21
Study Hall (178)	3,345.21

PER PUPIL COST

Study Hall (301)	$139.38
Study Hall (155)	101.37
Study Hall (178)	81.59
Study Hall (178)	58.68
Study Hall (178)	54.83
Study Hall (178)	47.78

If a school district has study halls, they should be calculated separately and not included in the cost of academic offerings.

Illus. 4-13

5

Discount Education vs. Convincing Subject Matter Outlays

Chapter IV dealt with grade level expenses within the school system. Now we will move on to the subject matter area costs within a school district. The value of knowing the exact cost of a particular subject taught at a particular grade level is obvious. How can we answer questions about how much handwriting costs to teach at the second grade if we do not have the exact figures with regard to teacher time allocations, materials, building space and overall miscellaneous costs involved in the production of a handwriting program? Since our analysis of school finance is sequential and each step depends upon the last step and the accuracy attached to the figures involved, it is expected that this accuracy be maintained through all phases of the development of our "CAS" system. Level V, just as all the previous levels, requires detailed accuracy.

Displaying Subject Matter Cost Concepts

When we look at the first, second, and third grade programs within a school system, how do we determine the cost allocations that should be applied to them? Remember, criticism from the public will come if our allocations do not have a firm logical foundation. In order to assure credible cost allocation, we turn to the state minimum standards for the development of an elementary education program. By using the state minimum time allocations, we guarantee that our program will at least represent what the state mandates in terms of an elementary school day. By utilizing the state mandated minimum standards or some standards which exceed these state mandated minimum standards, we guarantee that we will not be criticized for an inadequate program. This consideration becomes primary in determining the cost allocations to be attached to a given elementary program within the school district.

Illus. 5-1 shows a time allocation for a minimum elementary program. Let us consider the time allocations applied to the first grade, for example. Fifty minutes per week are utilized to develop the opening exercise of the school day. We then ask ourselves what percentage of the total fifteen hundred minute per week time allocation for the first grade does that fifty minutes represent? By determining this fact, we determine a base for the development of the cost which should be applied to the curricular practice of opening exercises. Once again, our time allocation of professional staff utilization becomes the key factor in determining the portion of time which should be allocated to each fiscal computation. By proceeding through the subject matter offered at each grade level, and by determining what percentage of time is utilized for each area of subject matter represented in the curriculum, it is possible to determine the portion of the total school day which is represented by that element of the subject matter. Once this proportion has been determined, it is applicable to the total cost for providing that subject matter during a particular period of time. Once the proportion has been applied, a cost breakdown is inevitable. The accuracy of the figures arrived at in the cost breakdown is directly dependent upon the accuracy of the time allocation applied to that particular phase of the curriculum.

Illus. 5-1 exhibits the combination usage of a total cost project for the first grade and an itemization of the time allocations utilized within the school system by first grade teachers. Once again, all this data is based logically upon the foundation provided by the state mandated minimum standards.

Notice also that the cost of the Kindergarten Program, ninety percent of which is state supported, has been itemized separately. Other programs within the school system could possibly fall into a category which would necessitate itemization. If this should be the case, then the most acceptable format for a particular school system would be the best format for public display. At this point, we should note that a breakdown of programs utilized in a fiscal analysis should be compatible with the goals and objectives of the school system.

When developing a cost analysis for a middle school or a junior high school, program emphasis must be considered. The number of subjects again becomes the primary factor in developing accuracy within your calculations. The number of minutes each teacher spends on each subject matter area becomes the proportional factor which is considered and applied to the overall cost of establishing that particular subject matter area. An in-system cost breakdown is acceptable, however, in the case of the state

ANYTOWN'S COST ACCOUNTABILITY
ELEMENTARY LEVEL LISTING
OF THE 19-- PROJECTED APPROPRIATIONS

KINDERGARTEN:

The Anytown School District Kindergarten Program for the 19-- Fiscal year will be held during two and one-half hour sessions. Kindergarten provides students with an introduction to the curriculum areas of reading, health and safety, social studies and mathematics.

The cost of this program is $99,096.99, ninety per cent (90%) which is state supported and ten per cent (10%), or $9,909.69, from local taxes.

ELEMENTARY:

	Average Minutes Per Week			
Grade	1st	2nd	3rd	4th, 5th
Opening Exercises	50	50	50	75
Reading	600	600	450	300
Language Development	150			
Language	---	250	350	225
Handwriting	100			
Mathematics	150	150	150	200
Social Studies	90	90	120	200
Science and Health	60	60	80	200
Art	60	55	60	80
Music	60	60	70	80
Physical Education	30	60	70	80
Recess	150	125	100	60
TOTAL	1500	1500	1500	1500

PROJECTED APPROPRIATIONS	$287,938.18	$303,766.22	$298,864.15	4th $261,127.82 5th $308,683.19

The above figures include the total projected costs of operating the described programs as outlined. These figures include every cost associated with the operations of these programs.

Illus. 5-1

mandated minimum standards for a junior high school program, or in the case of a middle school, a combination of the standards of a middle school and junior high school program is more acceptable. These standards have been carefully considered at the state level and represent state law in terms of what is required as a minimum program of instruction within the school system. It is more logical and credible to assume that a program developed and mandated at the state level would be more acceptable to a local population, in terms of justification, than a program developed within the school district. However, some school districts have a sophisticated process of curriculum development, and if this is a fact within your school system, then, probably, the program that you have developed would be more acceptable to your constituency. Whichever the case may be, be sure to choose that system of organizational structure which can be best justified in terms of the rationale behind the philosophy of your particular educational program. Notice that in Illus. 5-2, a brief explanation of the program precedes the cost analysis. Also, consider that the intramural program and special curriculum areas are explained separately, not as a part of the normal curricular offerings. Once again, deviance from this pattern is acceptable if a deviation suits the needs in organizational structure of the system which you are developing. All in all, a sophisticated cost analysis of any school program offers only a barometer of value by which one may measure the effectiveness of the instructional program offered. This barometer of value becomes a key factor in understanding the priorities

ANYTOWN'S COST ACCOUNTABILITY
MIDDLE SCHOOL LISTING
OF THE 19-- PROJECTED APPROPRIATIONS

Boys and girls in early adolescence face many new, emotional, physical, intellectual, social, and moral problems. We believe the middle school organization should create an atmosphere in which each youth can be helped to recognize his strengths and weaknesses, grow in self understanding, and be encouraged to express himself in the light of these understandings so that his best efforts are displayed as an individual and as a member of our society.

THE MIDDLE SCHOOL PROGRAM:

The Middle School Program for the 19   Fiscal year will include directed instruction in the areas listed below:

Sixth Grade: (Self-contained classrooms), Projected Cost: $265,286.39

English	Science-Health	Music
Reading	Social Studies	Physical Education
Spelling	Art	

Seventh Grade: (Block-time classes), Projected Cost: $255,686.31

Language Arts-Social Studies	Industrial Arts
Mathematics-Science and Health	Home Economics
Art	Physical Education
Music	

Eighth Grade: (Departmentalized classes), Projected Cost: $259,791.86

Language Arts	Mathematics	Art
American History	Industrial Arts	Music
Science-Health	Home Economics	Physical Education

On a voluntary basis, students will have the opportunity to participate in special music groups at each grade level. Intramural sports will be available for boys and girls interested, and there will be an interscholastic sports program available to boys in grades seven and eight.

Illus. 5-2

established by the school system. Without some measure of detail within the instructional program, the generalities upon which a student's progress is based are not sufficient to justify the expense and effort required by the instructional process. Complete accuracy in determining this barometer of value will insure its credibility within the community and determine its effectiveness as a representative of administrative efficiency within the school district. A 5 percent margin of error should be maintained constantly throughout the first year of the program's development. After the first year, the margin of error will be determined by the accuracy of the calculations as the program becomes more sophisticated.

Creative Formula Calculations

Illus. 5-3 represents the conversion formula for converting costs from grade level to subject matter. Once again, both teacher time allocation and student enrollment affect the formulation of the new cost figures. To break the various curricular area dollar appropriations into dollar amounts for specific subjects, first it is necessary to calculate anticipated enrollment for the area and then establish the percentage of enrollment each subject represents. Once this operation is completed, you simply multiply the percentage by the appropriations figure. The result is the cost of that particular subject matter area of the curriculum. As we examine closely Illus. 5-3, we realize that it is also necessary to include specific cost factors for plant operation and plant maintenance. Student activities must be determined and translated in terms of a cost ratio. Building administration must be allocated according to the number of students served by the building administration. And if a learning resource center is available within the building, that function, also, must be appropriated on a proportional basis to the total cost of the school program.

Once again, the formulation of the conversion formula figures is dependent upon the accuracy of the percentage ratios, as determined by the time allocation applied to the professional staff involved in that particular subject matter area. Once these time allocations have been accurately determined on the basis of students served within the building, accuracy is guaranteed for the final cost calculations.

Weighting, once again, is an important factor in the determination of an accurate analysis of the high school program cost. Here again, courses such as language arts, which enroll a large number of students, and also employ a large number of teachers, need no weighting factor. However, other subject matter areas, such as vocational agriculture, which might employ only one teacher, would need weighting. This weighting is accomplished by merely adjusting the calculated cost of offering that particular

ANYTOWN HIGH SCHOOL
"CAS" CONVERSION FORMULA
LEVEL IV TO V

I.   To break the various curricular areas designated dollar appropriations into dollar amounts for specific subjects (1) Calculate anticipated enrollment for the area, (2) then establish the percentage of enrollment for each subject. Multiply the per cent by the appropriations figure.

Example—Foreign Language ($44,463.90)
enrollment 450 = 100%

Latin I—	60 =	13%
Latin II—	60 =	13%
Spanish I—	120 =	28%
Spanish II—	60 =	13%
French I—	90 =	20%
French II—	60 =	13%
	450	100%

of $44,463.90

II.   Plant Operations and Plant Maintenance:

    a.   Number of sections in each subject × Estimated factor =
        Power factor for room size (scale 1-8)

    b.   Add the number factors.

    c.   Divide the appropriations of maintenance and operations by the total factor.

    d.   Multiply each factor by maintenance dollar figure.
        Multiply each factor by operations dollar figure.

III.   Student Activity:

Determine the power figure by number of class sections used to handle the enrollment.

Class size × number of sections × times met per week

IV.   Building Administration:

Class size × times met per week × number of sections = factor

Illus. 5-3

V.   Transportation:

Class size × times met per week × number of sections = factor

VI.   Learning Resource Center:

Class size × meetings per week × number of sections = factor

Illus. 5-3 *(Con't.)*

course by the actual salary of the personnel involved in that course. For example, if you find that your vocational agriculture program costs a total of seven thousand dollars, and at the same time you know that the instructors salary alone equals fourteen thousand dollars, then you know that you need a seven thousand dollar weight factor added to the calculation representing the cost of vocational agriculture. This weight factor should then be deducted from the most costly program offered in the school. For example, if your seven thousand dollar weight factor is added to vocational agriculture, then it should also be deducted from the total cost appropriation for the language arts department, thus equalizing the total allocation for the entire building. There is an internal dependency between cost-weight-ratio and program cost factors. The accurate determination of these considerations is the only guarantee to credibility and validity of the process.

Illustrations and Explanations for People

Illus. 5-4 refers to a complete cost breakdown of the senior high school program. The number of sections are listed along with the course titles, and after each course title a projected cost figure. This could represent an appropriation for that particular course for a given school year. Notice also the differences in cost between various programs within the curriculum. It is usually inspiring to most administrators to find that some of the traditional programs, which have been considered expensive, are not necessarily the most costly within the curriculum. Point of reference would be Latin I, which, as you can see, has a fairly average unit cost or section cost. Compare this to physics, which has a section cost of approximately one thousand dollars less. A close analysis of the various projected section costs will expose the true financial burden of the school system, while at the same time, justify changes in next year's appropriations.

Other factors may be discovered by closely analyzing a cost breakdown of the entire senior high school program. Some courses, such as

ANYTOWN'S COST ACCOUNTABILITY
SENIOR HIGH SCHOOL LISTING
OF THE COURSE LEVEL 19-- PROJECTED APPROPRIATIONS

COURSE TITLE	NO. SECT.	PROJECTED COST	COURSE TITLE	NO. SECT.	PROJECTED COST
Vocational Agriculture I	1	$ 6,574.31	Home Ec. I	5	23,613.82
Vocational Agriculture II	1	6,574.31	Home Ec. II	3	14,363.19
Art I	3	15,672.09	Industrial Arts	9	38,017.49
Art II	2	10,448.03	Engineering Drawing	1	3,169.33
Banking	1	2,819.36	Algebra I	10	38,557.81
Business Law	1	4,438.58	Algebra II	5	19,737.58
Business Arithmetic	3	13,331.33	General Math L	3	12,758.58
Bookkeeping	3	8,783.16	General Math R	7	25,798.56
Business Off. Ed. (I.O.E.)	5	13,300.43	Geometry	7	25,798.56
General Business	5	15,722.24	Advanced Math	1	4,864.87
Economics	1	5,093.44	Honors Math	1	4,864.87
Salesmanship	1	5,093.43	Varsity Band	1	7,835.08
Typing I	5	24,520.87	Junior Band	1	5,112.39
Typing II	5	24,520.87	Orchestra	1	3,841.81
English 9 Low	3	6,611.57	Senior Choir	1	8,379.62
English 9 Regular	10	45,231.64	9th Grade Choir	1	4,023.33
English 9 Honors	1	4,220.65	Health	7	41,398.84
English 10 L	3	12,661.94	Earth Science L	1	3,513.06
English 10 R	10	45,231.64	Earth Science R	9	29,552.23
English 10 H	1	4,220.65	Biology I L	2	7,025.57
English 11 L	3	12,661.94	Biology I R	14	42,986.18
English 11 R	7	30,300.80	Biology II	5	15,526.72
English 11 H	1	4,220.65	Chemistry	4	13,020.03
English 12 R	8	36,034.04	Physics	1	3,513.06
English 12 H	1	4,220.65	Physiology	4	13,020.07
Journalism I & II	2	4,220.65	Senior Social Studies	10	38,773.10
Latin I	2	8,171.23	9th Grade Social Studies	2	7,267.32
Latin II	2	8,171.23	World History	9	31,076.49
Spanish I	4	17,636.81	American History	12	41,978.85
Spanish II	2	8,373.78	Geo-Politics	1	2,820.85
French I	3	12,782.98	Driver Ed.	3	13,331.33
French II, III, & IV	2	8,373.78	Special Ed.	2	2,714.57
Physical Ed. 9	5	28,262.62	TOTAL		$1,035,019.47
Physical Ed. 10	5	28,262.61			

The cost of one section of the above listed courses may be calculated by dividing the total cost for that course by the number of existing sections. For example:
$8,171.23 (Cost of Latin I) ÷ 2 (Number of sections) = $4,085.61 (Cost of one section of Latin I)

Illus. 5-4

banking, have a very low section cost, while other courses, such as junior band, have a relatively high section cost. By formulating a value judgement as to which program is of more benefit to students, it is possible to compare program offerings with program expense. This comparison provides a very complete, accurate, empirical analysis of current spending patterns. This factual analysis can be of unending value to the school administrator who, on a daily basis, must explain why certain amounts of funds are expended on certain programs. Moreover, a school administrator knows exactly how much it costs to produce one course within the curriculum, which before was a little known current fact. These facts alone can justify involvement in a cost accountability system. A sophistication of these facts can establish a well justified financial foundation for the development of a program with continuity and involvement throughout the school system.

Behavioral Objectives as Selling Agents

Illus. 5-5 provides a simplified view of the crosswalk concept used to convert grade level costs into subject matter costs. Horizontally, it is necessary to list only the grade level and the total cost for that grade level, while vertically on the scale, the various program components of the school day are listed. Thus, by completing a careful study of the allocation of professional staff time to the various functions represented by the subject matter within a grade level, it is possible to develop an accurate analysis of subject matter cost. This crosswalk concept has been utilized continuously throughout the different stages of "CAS" development. The purpose of the crosswalk is simply to provide a vehicle by which you may systematically develop a proportional cost breakdown of subject matter within grade levels.

"CROSSWALK CONCEPT" CONVERSION
CHART FOR GRADE LEVEL COSTS TO
SUBJECT MATTER AREA COSTS WITHIN GRADE LEVELS
(LEVEL IV TO LEVEL V)

SUBJECT	GRADE 1	GRADE 2	GRADE 3	TOTAL
Opening School Day	$100.	$50.	$100.	$250.
Art	$100.	$100.	$100.	$300.
Music	$100.	$100.	$100.	$300.
Physical Education	$100.	$100.	$100.	$300.
Reading	$100.	$200.	$300.	$600.
	$500.	$550.	$700.	$1750.

Illus. 5-5

A properly implemented cost accountability system will enable each school district to take advantage of more concrete and specific data relevant to administrative decisions, spell out more completely the objectives of educational programs, and analyze systematically alternative educational programs.

The "CAS" system will also: Evaluate thoroughly the benefits and costs of educational programs.

Produce total, rather than partial, cost estimates of educational programs.

Present, on a multi-year basis, the prospective cost in anticipated accomplishments of educational programs.

Review objectives and conduct educational program analysis on a continuing, year-round basis, instead of a quick review only made to meet budget deadlines.

A cost accountability system provides a new approach to an old problem—that of better utilization of our limited resources to improve the learning process.

To assure that education continues to hold a priority for expenditure of tax resources, in the light of the American taxpayer's demand for justification of the use of his tax dollar, school officials are beginning to utilize a cost accountability system as a new decision making tool to communicate more clearly the necessity and justification for expenditures.

The "CAS" system is made up of objectives plus dollars, which equal a goal oriented budget. At this point, a rhetorical question might be: how does a school tie dollars to objectives?

For several years, teachers across the nation have been developing performance objectives, and now for the first time, many school systems are attempting to interpret these objectives in terms of dollars.

Within this new accountability procedure, costs are determined by the various types of instructional programs offered. The system incorporates both district-wide and individual school goals and objectives. Buildings may differ because needs and priorities may vary with each group of students. For example, here is how one of the staples of instruction, language arts, is described in the new accountability system behavioral objectives:

> *District Goal*—To provide a program of instruction and an educational setting designed to enable each student to learn as much as possible and to develop the skills, knowledge and the capacity for making responsible decisions for his own life, and to provide a means for every educator to assist students in reaching this goal.
>
> *Administrative Goal*—The percentage of pupils achieving the school system objectives should increase at each "grade" level, and program em-

phasis should be extended into other levels to accommodate needs of pupils who participated in the program previously.

District Objective—Seventy-two percent of students in grade one will achieve at the 1.6 grade equivalent by the end of the school year, as measured by the Standard Achievement Test.

School Objective—Seventy-five percent of the children will achieve one month's growth for one month's instruction in the language arts program during the second semester of the school year, as measured by the Standard Achievement Test, Reader's Digest Test, Science Program Textbooks and teacher made tests.

School Objective—By the end of the school year, 80 percent of the students participating in a Reading Program will achieve 1.0 months of reading achievement for each month in the reading program during the school year, as measured by the standardized test.

These objectives cover only one part of the primary language arts program for the district in two of its schools. In preparing these objectives, school administrators must work very closely with the teaching staff directly involved in program implementation. A series of in-service training sessions, covering basic concepts of accountability, behavioral objectives, writing, and budget coding systems must be held for principals and selected teachers who will be involved in the development of an accountability system.

Each school and department must then prepare from one to ten behavioral performance objectives for each program. Later, accountability personnel should meet with budgetary units to review objectives and project costs. At the end of the academic year, the staff will evaluate the objectives and make adjustments to program for the next year on the basis of their evaluation.

The accountability system will undergo changes each year, as some objectives will need to be defined more precisely while others will have to be rewritten. Preparation time should be expanded so that the staff will begin work on the next school year's objectives early in October. Evaluation criteria and procedures should also be defined at this time.

The desired result will be a budgetary system which units performance objectives and dollars more closely than the current fiscal system. This will enable the school district to evaluate their return on the money invested in public education.

The following are the basic elements of "CAS."

A goal is a statement of broad direction, purpose or intent based on the value system of the community. A goal is general and timeless, and it is not concerned with a specific achievement within a specified period of time.

Objectives are desired accomplishments which can be measured within a given time span. Achievement of an objective advances the system toward the corresponding goal. Accordingly, objectives must be developed to support and contribute to the achievement of established goals.

Programs are defined as a group of interdependent, closely related activities progressing toward a common objective. It is a package of related activities.

A program structure is a hierarchical arrangement of programs which demonstrates the relationship between activities, goals, and objectives. The structure contains categories of activities with common output objectives.

Illus. 5-6 shows the process of progression from a system philosophy, to departmental goals, and then to a given teacher's objective within the classroom. Many school systems have spent countless hours developing detailed behavioral objectives for each department within each subject matter area in the school system. In general, behavioral objectives for one school are very similar to the same types of behavioral changes desired by another school system. For this reason, it is more expeditious to utilize the general pattern of behavioral objective development, rather than to redesign a custom made set of behavioral objectives for your school system. There are available many sets of behavioral objectives. Without endorsing any particular set, it should be noted that with sufficient research, it is possible to find a set of behavioral objectives which suitably fits the needs of the philosophy under which the school system is presently operating. When such a set of objectives has finally been identified by a representative group of staff members who, in the final analysis, will be using them, the school system has saved a tremendous amount of financial outlay. Although behavioral objectives should not be thought of as an end in themselves, they should be considered a means to the end of developing a fiscal system of accountability which maximizes the fiscal credibility of the instructional program. Once the sought after behavioral objectives have been identified, and the cost for achieving those objectives has been fixed, the school system will be prepared and equipped to move toward a more credible curriculum justification.

The program budget in a cost accountability system is a statement of policy that relates cost to goals, objectives, and programs based upon a subject matter classification. When the goals and objectives of a school district have been defined and the programs to meet those objectives have been documented, the estimated cost of those programs must be reported in the accounting budget. Together the philosophy, goals, and objectives of the school system justify the expenditure of tax dollars for the achievement of learning for boys and girls within the school system. In this way

DEFINITIONS OF TERMS

I.   PHILOSOPHY: A composite statement based upon beliefs, concepts, and attitudes, from which the educational purpose of the district is designed.

Ex.:   We believe that the schools should foster basic individual development in various aspects of living: physical, social and moral.

II.   GOAL: A statement that proposes desired and valued competencies, states of being, and general levels of proficiency to be achieved. Goals are achieved through the accomplishment of specific objectives.

Ex.:   Develop an understanding of political, economic, and social patterns of the world.

III.   OBJECTIVE: An observable and sometimes quantifiable achievement accomplished under specific conditions. Objectives should reflect all the critical factors required for the achievement of a goal.

Ex.:   (Student Performance Objective) When presented with a statement regarding a controversial issue, the student will seek out and examine at least two other viewpoints, and then state the final opinion regarding the issue.

Illus. 5-6

instructional programs, students, and tax money come together to form the school system. The end result of this process is credible education.

Objectives, then, represent measurable achievements, the attainment of which advances the school system in the direction of established goals. Documented, delineate objectives are almost nonexistent in public school districts. Existing statements of philosophy contain few items of a quantifiable nature, and they are not projected within a time frame. Integral to meaningful objectives are the evaluative criteria by which the effectiveness of programs in attaining objectives will be measured. It will be observed that each of the objectives formulated over a period of time will necessitate revision and development.

Measuring program effectiveness is the most difficult problem encountered in the development of an accountability system. The systems that have been established in school districts for measuring objectives, other than standardized tests, are usually inadequate and poorly constructed.

Public Appeal and Results at This Level

It is recognized that there are areas of the total educational process which are not evaluated quantitatively. Most of these unique or special areas could be subjectively evaluated, but documented subjective evaluation is difficult and in many cases nonexistent. There are very few successful subjective evaluations on file in school districts. Although this is a difficult area requiring significant effort, there is general agreement among educators that this type of evaluative criterion is necessary and can be developed. Therefore, it is suggested that whenever possible, the very best standardized instrument be used for evaluating the achievement of students within a given program. Standardized tests should be identified which possess a high degree of validity and reliability, and which have been proven by time to be useful instruments in the measurement of student achievement. Again, it is more logical to assume that the validity of an instrument based upon many thousands of users is more convincing to the public than a homemade or teacher made instrument based upon one or two classrooms. The primary purpose of our process is to develop a credible method of associating school finance with achievement. Teacher made instruments are an alternative, but are not acceptable toward gaining this goal. New systems, such as CAM and SPED, have been developed to attempt, in a logical, progressive way, to identify objectives and attach cost to them. However, these are in developmental stages and are not available for mass consumption at this time. It is more logical to use instruments on the market which have been developed over a long period of time and have proven reliability for testing student achievement. If a system fails to use the proper instrument in measuring pupil progress, then it is inevitable that the credibility of their "CAS" system will be challenged. It remains difficult to defend an instrument which measures subjective pupil achievement, and its impossible to defend a teacher made instrument based upon a small population within one classroom. All instruments used must be the best available in the world of education today.

Our purpose is to coordinate the use of all quantitative methods of analyzing the educational process today.

How to Move On with "CAS"

In order to proceed with the development of the "CAS" system, it is essential to have an understanding of the information contained in Illus. 5-7, 5-8 and 5-9. Illus. 5-7 explains one method of coding designed for computer adaptation. However, if a coding system presently exists within the system, it is not essential that this system be used. Any coding system which meets the requirements of the financial process may be adapted to the "CAS" concept.

A SAMPLE CODING SYSTEM

	Level I[1]		Level II	Level III	Level IV	Level V (Opt.)
Object XX	Function XXX	Scope X	Program XX	Building XX	Grade XX	Course XXX
Example: A	16a	1	11	61	10	(to be developed)
Salary	Teachers Summer School	Regular	Math	Senior High School	10th Grade	Algebra I

Illus. 5-7

---

[1]Level I is state mandated accounting system.
Note: "X" indicates number of digits in code group.

COST ACCOUNTABILITY SYSTEM
LEVEL IV TO LEVEL V

BREAKDOWN FORMULAS—HIGH SCHOOL

(102,029.31 Grade 9)

Home Ec.	.045
Art I	.045
Practical Science	.091
General Science	.091
Algebra I	.091
General Math	.091
Girls Health & P.E.	.091
Spanish I	.046
Industrial Arts	.091
Latin I	.045
English 9	.136
Boys Health & P.E.	.091
General Business	.046

Sec. (22)

(87,310.33 Grade 10)

Home Ec. II	.047
English 10	.190
Plane Geometry	.048
Sr. Band	.048
Girls Health & P.E. 10	.048
Biology	.095
Spanish II	.047
World History	.095
World Geography	.048
Latin II	.047
Boys Health & P.E. 10	.049
Bookkeeping I	.095
Business Math	.048
Typing I	.095

Sec. (21)

(70,338.94 Grade 11)

Machine Shop I	.280
Home Ec. III	.040
Advanced Art	.040
English 11	.120
Chemistry	.080
Drivers Training	.120
Spanish III & IV	.040
Metal & Mach. Ind. Arts	.040
American History	.120
Shorthand I	.040
Algebra II	.040
Typing II	.040

Sec. (25)

(79,730.19 Grade 12)

Home Ec. IV	.029
Machine Shop II	.205
English 12	.030
Sr. Eng.	.058
Physics	.030
Sr. High Chorus	.030
D.E.	.205
Earth Science	.030
Advanced Biology	.030
Auto. Ind. Arts	.058
American Government	.088
Ec./Soc.	.030
Speech	.030
Journalism	.030
Personal Skills	.029
Office Practice	.030

Sec. (34)

Trigonometry	.029
Shorthand II	.029

Illus. 5-8

ELEMENTARY AND JR. HIGH SCHOOL
LEVEL IV TO LEVEL V
CONVERSION PERCENTAGES

Subject Area	K	1	2	3	4	5	6	7	8
				G R A D E S				JUNIOR HIGH	
1. Citizenship	.05	.05	.05	.05	.05	.05	.05		
2. Reading	.36	.36	.33	.30	.27	.24	.24		
3. Language	.03	.03	.03	.04	.06	.07	.07		
4. Spelling	.04	.04	.04	.04	.04	.04	.04		
5. Handwriting	.03	.03	.03	.05	.05	.05	.05		
6. Math	.13	.13	.14	.14	.14	.13	.13		
7. Social Studies	.04	.04	.05	.06	.06	.07	.07		
8. Science & Health	.05	.05	.06	.06	.09	.10	.10		
9. Dir. Phys. Ed.	.05	.05	.05	.05	.05	.06	.06		
10. Music	.05	.05	.05	.05	.05	.05	.05		
11. Art	.05	.05	.05	.05	.03	.03	.03		
12. Recess	.08	.08	.08	.08	.08	.08	.08		
13. Admin. Work	.04	.04	.04	.03	.03	.03	.03		
Junior High									
U. S. History								.16	.16
Science								.16	.16
Reading								.17	.17
English								.17	.17
Math								.17	.17
Creative Skills²								.17	.17

Illus. 5-9

²Creative Skills include Home Ec.—Ind. Arts—Phys. Ed.—Art—Guidance

6

Public Display of Discount Education

This section is dedicated to the design of a public relations brochure. The assimilation of the foregoing accountability information is only surpassed by its presentation to the public it serves. A complete organizational format has been designed, and it is presented in this chapter for your consideration and review. If a school system followed the format presented, they would compile a complete overview of the financial status of a school district. This brochure could be highlighted by photographs of various programs where large amounts of funds have been expended throughout the school district. Transportation could be highlighted in one section, while another might feature cafeteria expenditures. Still another section could be dedicated to various academic programs throughout the school system and the costs incurred for these programs. A booklet such as this becomes an annual report of the school district to the tax paying public. It provides a working compilation of materials which administrators and board members may refer to on a continuous basis throughout the school year. At the end of each calendar year, a new annual report may be developed along the lines of the original format. Revisions and adjustments may be made in line with the value system of the community. Using the format framework presented in this chapter for a guide, it is possible to save the cost of design consultants. Although this format will not serve each school district to an equal degree, it will serve in part all school districts.

Your contribution is to extract from the format the information which you feel would be most significant to the community you serve. Titles and subtitles may be changed at will, and information added or deleted as it best contributes to the overall explanation of your academic program. All of this information should be covered thoroughly with the staff and board of education, in order that they may present reasonable explanations of items included if approached with questions after the distribution of your system profile. If this information is new and organized in an unfamiliar format, much interpretation will be needed for the tax paying public. Therefore, a timetable or systematic approach, moving from the simple to the complex, should be adopted by your administrative staff. It is important that the first brochure include many photographs of students and leaders in the school district, thus insuring its acceptance among a few supporters. The internal administration and staff should be well oriented to the contents of the brochure and its purpose. Presentation of the material should be made at a formal board of education meeting in order to receive media treatment. Once the proper format and background information has been distributed, it will become the task of the administration to lead the community in an understanding of the complete contents. In some situations, this may involve a repeated number of many annual reports growing toward a combination of a complete statistical breakdown of the school system. Remember, most people understand courses such as mathematics, reading, writing, and social studies, but they find it extremely difficult to equate these with titles such as transportation, administration and instructional cost. It becomes our task to make every effort possible to explain, in the simplest form, the most complex concepts of the financial aspects of the school district. Keeping this in mind, we strive to develop a brochure which will be pleasing in appearance as well as uncomplicated in content. This becomes the polish on our project of developing accountable financing and credible spending within our school district. This represents our first efforts toward humanizing the statistical results of our accountability process. Since it is essential that the community we serve accept the facts we present, it is also equally essential that we humanize the content of our investigation in a format that is impossible to reject. This is the primary purpose for including the following annual report structure.

ANYTOWN BOARD OF EDUCATION
19-- ANNUAL REPORT

Symbol of School District

or

A Picture of the Buildings

BOARD OF EDUCATION

Here a list of
Board of Education Members

ADMINISTRATION

Here a list of
School Administrators

PREFACE

This report has been developed in an effort to explain to the taxpayers of Anytown how the Board of Education approaches the many
complexed problems involved in operating our schools. As these
figures indicate, we believe in a basic well-rounded educational
program based upon conservative and efficient spending. Our only
purpose is to provide the best possible education for the children
of Anytown within our available funds.

President, Board of Education

DESCRIPTION OF OUR COST ACCOUNTABILITY SYSTEM

Increasing public school expenditures have necessitated the search
for more effective and efficient ways to use available resources.
Clearly limited are the tax and manpower resources needed to support
public services. Because public education has been called upon to
solve many economic as well as social problems, expenditures for
education will continue to claim a significant share of the tax
dollar. But as these expenditures rise and available tax resources
are stretched, the public is demanding justification of educational
costs.

School officials have been able to report the transportation cost
per pupil, per bus and per route. Similarly we know the cost of
cleaning, heating or maintaining a school building, feeding a child
and running an athletic program. However, very few of us can tell
what it costs to raise a child's reading or computational skill to a

higher level; nor can we say if more or less should be spent to achieve
this new level in a longer or shorter time; nor are we sure if we are
communicating to the taxpayers these objectives in relation to costs.

Against this background, school officials are becoming more cognizant
of the need for a more responsive and timely system that will effectively communicate the costs of educational outputs. We need a system
that will allow for better decision making, alternative selections,
planning and forecasting. This cost accountability system appears
capable of meeting these needs.

With this system, school officials have better information for
planning educational programs and for making choices among the alternative ways in which funds can be allocated to achieve the school
district's established objectives, the programs to reach these objectives, the methods of evaluating the programs, and the cost of operating
them.

Superintendent, Anytown School District

```
┌─────────────────────────────────────────────────┐
│                                                 │
│                                                 │
│                                                 │
│          A Picture of the Board of Education    │
│                                                 │
│                                                 │
│                                                 │
│                                                 │
└─────────────────────────────────────────────────┘
```

ANNUAL APPROPRIATION RESOLUTION 19--

LINE ITEM	AMOUNT APPROPRIATED
1. Coordination[1]	$ 36,500.00
2. Instruction	599,500.00
3. Coordinated Activities	21,200.00
4. Auxiliary Services	46,120.00
5. Operation of School Plant	46,300.00
6. Special Services	1,800.00
7. Supplies	74,500.00
8. Materials for Maintenance	6,000.00
9. Equipment Replacements	14,800.00
10. Contract and Open Service	51,300.00
11. Fixed Charges	151,500.00
12. Contingent	7,200.00
13. Capital Outlay	23,000.00
14. General Fund Debt Service	70,200.00
GRAND TOTAL APPROPRIATIONS GENERAL FUND	1,149,920.00

*The above state mandated budgetary listing is difficult to understand because the division categories are unrelated to the instructional programs typically existing within Anytown and other school districts.

---

[1]Coordination—This includes all administrative expenses.

COST PER PUPIL PER YEAR - ELEMENTARY

SUBJECT	K[2]	1st	2nd	3rd
Citizenship (Pledge to flag, etc.)	54.56	52.62	53.74	52.40
Reading	392.85	378.86	354.68	314.43
Language	32.74	31.57	32.24	41.92
Spelling	43.65	42.10	42.99	41.92
Handwriting	32.74	31.57	32.24	52.40
Math	141.86	136.81	150.47	146.73
Social Studies	43.65	42.10	53.74	62.88
Science - Health	54.56	52.62	64.48	62.88
Directed Phys. Ed.	54.56	52.62	53.74	52.40
Music	54.56	52.62	53.74	52.40
Art	54.56	52.62	53.74	52.40
Recess	87.30	84.19	85.98	83.84
Admin. Work (Grades, Attendance)	43.65	42.10	42.99	31.44

COST PER PUPIL PER YEAR ELEMENTARY

SUBJECT	4th	5th	6th
Citizenship (Pledge to flag, etc.)	52.76	59.79	52.32
Reading	284.91	322.89	251.14
Language	63.31	71.75	73.25
Spelling	42.21	47.83	41.85
Handwriting	52.76	59.79	52.32
Math	147.73	167.43	136.03
Social Studies	63.31	71.75	73.25
Science - Health	94.97	107.63	104.64
Directed Phys. Ed.	52.76	59.79	62.78
Music	52.76	59.79	52.32
Art	31.65	35.87	31.39
Recess	84.41	95.67	83.71
Admin. Work (Grades, Attendance)	31.65	35.87	31.39

COST PER PUPIL PER YEAR - JR. HIGH

SUBJECT	7th	8th
U. S. History	167.15	167.37
Science	167.15	167.37
Reading	177.60	177.82
Math	177.60	177.82
Creative Skills	177.60	177.82
English	177.60	177.82

Teachers with more experience and more educational preparation are paid higher salaries, thus the above resulting cost differences.

---

[2]K—Kindergarten

ANYTOWN SCHOOLS' COST ACCOUNTABILITY SYSTEM
LISTING OF THE 19-- PROJECTED APPROPRIATIONS

Clerical Staff Pictures	Accounting Office Pictures

PROGRAMS BY SUBJECT   AMOUNT APPROPRIATED

1.	Vocational Agriculture	$ 11,936.74
2.	Art	128,458.98
3.	Business Education	95,493.96
4.	Learning Resource Centers.	46,435.24
5.	Language Arts.	1,029,052.45
6.	Foreign Language	54,324.00
7.	Physical Education	170,581.72
8.	Home Economics	59,683.73
9.	Industrial Arts.	60,309.03
10.	Mathematics	351,009.33
11.	Music.	123,520.79
12.	Science and Health	315,951.29
13.	Social Studies	310,947.56
14.	Student Activities (Sports, etc.).	51,246.97
15.	Coordination (Includes classroom administration)	238,702.20
16.	Child Study Center	226,240.93
17.	Kindergarten	89,509.25
18.	Driver Education	11,936.74

TOTAL PROJECTED 19-- APPROPRIATIONS $3,375,341.00

This listing of costs shows the projected expense of maintaining the above subject matter areas for the 19-- Fiscal Year. (From January 1, 19-- to December 31, 19--.)

Item fifteen, Coordination, includes the percentage of each teacher's salary which pays for lunch money collecting, attendance taking, and record keeping within each classroom, as well as all other administrative expenses related to normal operation. Also, the administrative costs for the Kindergarten Program are included under item fifteen, Coordination.

Ninety per cent (90%) of the Kindergarten Program cost is paid for from state support, the other ten per cent (10%) is paid from local taxes.

ANYTOWN'S COST ACCOUNTABILITY SYSTEM
LISTING BY BUILDING
OF THE 19-- PROJECTED APPROPRIATIONS

```
+-----------------------------+   +-----------------------------+
|                             |   |                             |
| Special Education Photographs|  | Typical Classroom Photographs|
|                             |   |                             |
+-----------------------------+   +-----------------------------+
```

BUILDINGS	AMOUNT APPROPRIATED
1. North Elementary	$ 159,972.30
2. Central Elementary	126,978.02
3. Columbia Elementary	222.757.31
4. June Elementary	212.866.49
5. East Elementary	214.632.74
6. South Elementary	215.574.83
7. July Elementary	176,952.15
8. April Elementary	91,633.35
9. West Elementary	138,129.36
10. Peach Middle School	421,915.76
11. Apple Middle School	353,848.80
12. Senior High School	1,035,019.47
TOTAL PROJECTED 19-- APPROPRIATIONS	$3,370,280.58

Buildings with larger student body enrollment are more expensive to operate.

Teachers with more experience and more educational preparation are paid higher salaries, thus the above resulting cost differences.

Pictures should express integration within the system.

ANYTOWN'S COST ACCOUNTABILITY
ELEMENTARY LEVEL LISTING
OF THE 19-- PROJECTED APPROPRIATIONS

Photographs of Cafeteria Program

Typical Instructional

Program Photograph

KINDERGARTEN:

The Anytown School District Kindergarten Program for the 19-- Fiscal
year will be held during two and one-half hour sessions. Kindergarten
provides students with an introduction to the curriculum areas of reading,
health and safety, social studies and mathematics.

The cost of this program is $99,096.99, ninety per cent (90%) which
is state supported and ten per cent (10%), or $9,909.69, from local taxes.

ELEMENTARY:

Average Minutes Per Week

Grade	1st	2nd	3rd	4th, 5th
Opening Exercises	50	50	50	75
Reading	600	600	450	300
Language Development	150	---	---	---
Language	---	250	350	225
Handwriting	100	---	---	---
Mathematics	150	150	150	200
Social Studies	90	90	120	200
Science and Health	60	60	80	200
Art	60	55	60	80
Music	60	60	70	80
Physical Education	30	60	70	80
Recess	150	125	100	60
TOTAL	1500	1500	1500	1500

PROJECTED	$287,938.18		$298,864.15	4th $261,127.82
APPROPRIATIONS		$303,766.22		5th $308,683.19

The above figures include the total projected costs of operating
the described programs as outlined. These figures include every cost
associated with the operations of these programs.

ANYTOWN'S COST ACCOUNTABILITY
MIDDLE SCHOOL LISTING
OF THE 19-- PROJECTED APPROPRIATIONS

Boys and girls in early adolescence face many new, emotional, physical, intellectual, social, and moral problems. We believe the middle school organization should create an atmosphere in which each youth can be helped to recognize his strengths and weaknesses, grow in self understanding, and be encouraged to express himself in the light of these understandings so that his best efforts are displayed as an individual and as a member of our society.

THE MIDDLE SCHOOL PROGRAM

The Middle School Program for the 19-- Fiscal year will include directed instruction in the areas listed below:

Sixth Grade: (Self-contained classrooms), Projected Cost: $265,286.39

English	Science-Health	Music
Reading	Social Studies	Physical Education
Spelling	Art	

Seventh Grade: (Block-time classes), Projected Cost: $255,686.31

Language Arts-Social Studies	Industrial Arts
Mathematics-Science and Health	Home Economics
Art	Physical Education
Music	

Eighth Grade: (Departmentalized classes), Projected Cost: $259,791.86

Language Arts	Mathematics	Art
American History	Industrial Arts	Music
Science-Health	Home Economics	Physical Education

On a voluntary basis, students will have the opportunity to participate in special music groups at each grade level. Intramural sports will be available for boys and girls interested, and there will be an interscholastic sports program available to boys in grades seven and eight.

```
+---------------------------------+    +---------------------------------+
|                                 |    |                                 |
|   Photographs of the District's |    |    Photographs of the           |
|      Transportation System      |    |    Cafeteria Program            |
|                                 |    |       in Operation              |
|                                 |    |                                 |
+---------------------------------+    +---------------------------------+
```

Design action pictures with students and staff involved.

WHY FISCAL PLANNING FOR THE PUBLIC SCHOOLS IS COMPLICATED!

Fiscal Planning Year

January 1 ———————————————————— December 31

Sept. $\dfrac{\text{1st School Year}}{\text{January 1, 19--}}$ June   Sept. $\dfrac{\text{2nd School Year}}{\text{December 31, 19--}}$ June

FACTORS TO CONSIDER:

1. Funds must be appropriated for the period from January 1 to December 31.

2. Funds must be budgeted for the period from July 1 to June 30.

3. Children attend school from September to June.

4. Every school year involves two different fiscal years.

5. Teachers are contracted for a 184 day school year from September to June.

6. Teachers' salaries must be paid from two different fiscal years.

7. Staff salaries represent 70% to 80% of all operating expenses of the school district.

8. It is extremely difficult to adjust programs at mid-year in January when the new fiscal period starts, because of teacher contract obligations assumed in September.

9. Public schools receive funds from local taxes, State taxes and Federal taxes all of which have different collection procedures and are re-distributed to our schools according to different formulas during the four fiscal quarters of the year. All of which means that it is complicated to know exactly what funds are available, and when.

PER PUPIL COST PER YEAR—HIGH SCHOOL

COURSE TITLE	GRADE	COST	COURSE TITLE	GRADE	COST
Latin I	9	$ 459.13	Spanish III & IV	11	$ 255.77
Woodworking, Ind. Arts	9	371.38	Chemistry	11	225.08
Home Ec. I	9	306.08	Drivers Training	11	183.49
General Science	9	273.07	Metal, Machine, Ind. Arts	11	140.67
Algebra I	9	257.90	English	11	136.13
Art I	9	241.64	American History	11	125.98
Practical Science	9	232.11	Algebra II	11	117.23
Girls Health & P. E.	9	197.54	Machine Shop II	12	1,816.07
Spanish I	9	185.69	Shorthand II	12	1,156.09
English 9	9	182.57	Distributive Education	12	778.31
General Math	9	182.05	Personal Skills	12	330.31
General Business	9	151.39	Physics	12	265.76
Home Ec. II	10	455.95	Special Education	12	257.32
Latin II	10	373.05	Home Ec. IV	12	256.90
Spanish II	10	315.66	Trig./Advanced Math	12	256.90
Bookkeeping I	10	267.56	Automotives - Ind. Arts	12	243.38
Plane Geometry	10	209.54	Office Practice	12	239.19
Biology	10	180.31	Speech	12	217.44
World Geography	10	174.62	Earth Science	12	170.85
English 10	10	171.02	Economics/Sociology	12	159.46
World History	10	169.27	Advanced Biology	12	140.70
Business Math	10	161.18	Journalism	12	119.59
Typing I	10	159.50	Senior English	12	85.63
Senior Band	10	110.28	American Government	12	85.56
Girls Phys. Ed.	10	99.78	English 12	12	70.35
Boys Phys. Ed.	10	61.11	Sr. High Chorus	12	46.90
Machine Shop I	11	1,230.93	Study Hall (301)		139.38
Shorthand I	11	562.71	Study Hall (155)		101.37
Home Ec. III	11	401.93	Study Hall (178)		81.59
Typing II	11	401.93	Study Hall (178)		58.68
Advanced Art	11	312.61	Study Hall (178)		54.83
Boys Phys. Ed., Health	9	185.69	Study Hall (178)		47.78

VOCATIONAL PROGRAMS—PER PUPIL COST PER YEAR

D.C.T. Diversified Co-op Training	$ 203.00
G.W.E. Occupational Work Experience	173.28
Child Care	139.67
Cosmetology I	125.00
Graphic Arts	124.99
D.C.T. Diversified Co-op Training	119.90
C.O.E. Co-op Office Experience	99.98
Production Agriculture	93.18

The above figures include the total projected costs of operating the
described programs as outlined. These figures include every cost associated with the operations of these programs.

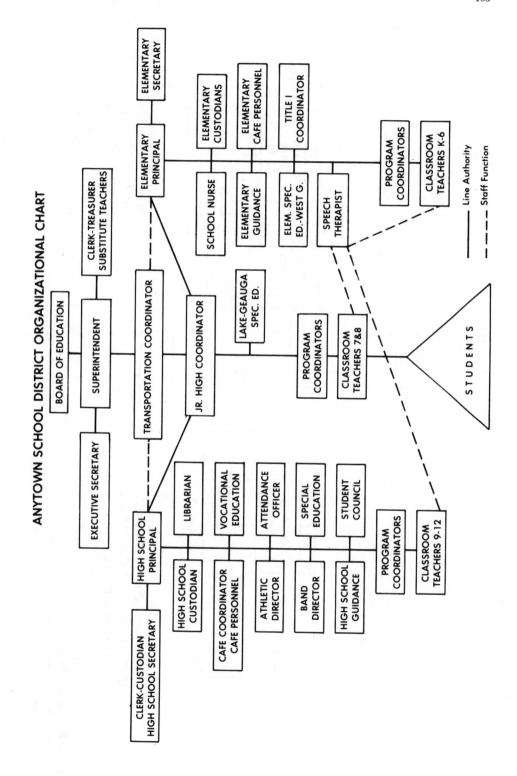

ANYTOWN SCHOOL DISTRICT ORGANIZATIONAL CHART

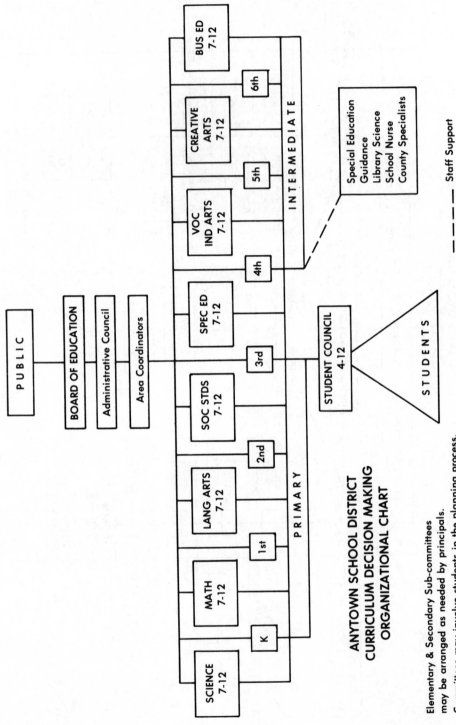

ANYTOWN SCHOOL DISTRICT
CURRICULUM DECISION MAKING
ORGANIZATIONAL CHART

Elementary & Secondary Sub-committees
may be arranged as needed by principals.
Committees may involve students in the planning process.

– – – – – Staff Support

ANYTOWN SCHOOL DISTRICT
FACTUAL DATA

Transportation:

1. We own and operate ten busses. Nine on a full-time basis, with one reserve.

2. Our total yearly mileage exceeds 88,000 miles.

Income and Millage:

Inside millage - guaranteed	4.50
Outside millage - voted	37.90
Total operating	42.40
Bond retirement - voted	9.00
Total millage	51.40

1973 APPRAISED VALUATION

Real estate	$11,108,270.00
Public utilities	1,416,900.00
Tangible personal property	2,000,000.00
Total	$14,525,170.00

ASSETS

High school and new elementary	$ 2,360,000.00
Contents	300,000.00
Land (cost)	28,957.00
Busses (Approximate value)	75,000.00

PAYROLL (average)

Administrative & non-teaching bi-weekly	$ 5,638.17
Teaching staff bi-monthly	25,036.80
All monthly	62,000.00

$62,000.00 x 12 = $744,000.00 approximate yearly

Cafeteria:

	72-73	71-72
Students served yearly	50,540	28,175
Labor expense	$21,720	$19,548

Basic menus include:

1. Pizza
2. Spaghetti
3. Weiners
4. Sloppy Joe's
5. Sliced Turkey
6. Hamburgers
7. Fish
8. Macaroni & Cheese
9. Roast Chicken

LIST OF PROJECTS COMPLETED SINCE AUGUST 19--

1. Completion of new elementary building.
2. Driveway re-surfacing.
3. Enclosed bleachers on stadium.
4. Siliconing front of old building.
5. Electrical re-wiring of old building.
6. Enclosure of boiler room work area.
7. Enlargement of sewer facilities.
8. Completion of fencing project.
9. Completion of library re-modeling.
10. Installation of new windows on second and third floors.
11. Completion of new Board of Education offices.
12. Negotiation of 2-1/2 year teachers contract.
13. Development of a line and staff organization.
14. Development of a curriculum decision-making organizational procedure.
15. Improvement of staff evaluation procedure.
16. Installation of new junior high lockers.
17. Complete cafeteria menu survey.
18. Purchase of new cafeteria equipment.
19. Sanctioned official clubs and organizations.
20. Started a self-help program for clubs in the school.
21. Provided custodial jobs for high school boys.
22. Earned enough money in cafeteria to purchase additional equipment.
23. Re-wired machine shop to meet national codes.
24. Painted inside of building.
25. Purchased two new busses.
26. Received approval from State for two additional special education units.
27. Refinished floors in three-story structure.
28. Completed plastering around window.project.
29. Sponsored a drug education program in the community.
30. Passed a renewal operating levy.
31. Installed new blinds and drapes where needed.
32. Developed a new science lab facility.
33. Developed two baseball diamonds.
34. Revised the present dress code.
35. Started new inventory controls on all equipment and materials
    used in the school including gasoline, food supplies, telephones,
    maintenance supplies and classroom equipment.
36. Started new security rules on locking up building & equipment.
37. Developed a detailed cost analysis of the entire system.
38. Completed all required State forms and reports.
39. Expanded the bus service.
40. Completed a revision of the Board of Education Policy Manual.
41. Installation of flasher lights.
42. Installation of parking system.
43. Developed Administrative Regulations.

Building Maintenance: High School   Elementary

    Average custodial hours per week   226   76
    Average total cost per week $577.40 $271.83

Student custodians are paid $1.69 per hour. This plan helps create jobs
for local students, while at the same time teaching them the responsibility
of maintaining the school.

SPECIAL EDUCATION CENTER
ORGANIZATIONAL CHART

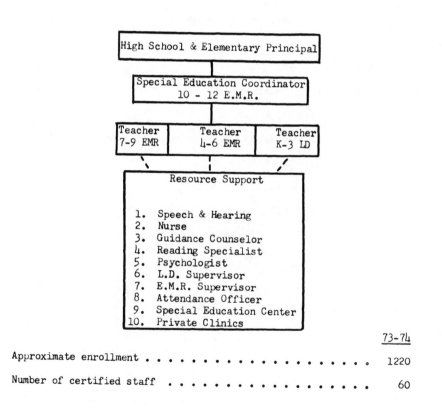

                                                        73-74

Approximate enrollment 1220

Number of certified staff   60

RECEIPTS

53% Local Tax

43% State School Foundation

3% Federal Government

1% Miscellaneous

EXPENDITURES

21.06% Language Arts - English - Spelling - Reading - Writing

10% Mathematics

9% Science & Health (including Drug Education)

8% Social Studies

5.6% Machine Shop

5.6% Special Education

5.1% Physical Education

5.1% Records - Grades - Attendance - Testing

4.8% Student Activities

3.9% Art

3.8% Music

3.8% Business Education

3% Home Economics

2.9% Kindergarten

2.7% Distributive Education

2.2% Library

1.8% Industrial Arts

1.5% Foreign Languages

.04% Drivers Education

PREVIEW OF FUTURE COST

REPORTING TECHNIQUES!

The following is a comparison of the Guidance Department's Report on Anytown High School Graduates and the Cost of Providing the Desired Training Indicated.

Area Studied		Students' Goals	Our Cost	How We Spend
1. College Bound		58%	$631,361.88	61%
2. Technical 8% Business 6% Nursing 2%		16%	$196,653.70	19%
3. Immediate Employment		12%	$ 93,151.75	9%
4. Armed Services 4% Marriage 3% Travel & Undecided 7%		14%	$113,852.14	11%
		100%	$1,035,019.47[3]	100%

```
┌─────────────────────────────────────────┐
│                                         │
│     Photographs of students actually    │
│                                         │
│     involved at Anytown High School     │
│                                         │
│                                         │
│                                         │
│                                         │
└─────────────────────────────────────────┘
```

---

[3]This figure represents the total cost of operating the present program at the Anytown Senior High School for one complete school year. (Including 3 months summer maintenance.)

AN ACHIEVEMENT

COST INDEX ANALYSIS!

Test Instruments Included

Stanford Achievement Test - Grade 6 Level, Based upon 460,000 Sixth Grade Students, Nationwide Reliability Determined to be 88% Copyright Date

Comprehensive Tests of Basic Skills - Grade 6 Level, Based upon 170,000 Sixth Grade Students, Nationwide Reliability Determined to be 93% Copyright Date

The Anytown School District standardized testing program is designed to compare the achievement of Anytown students at the Kindergarten, 4th, 6th, 8th and 10th grade levels with the achievement of students of those levels throughout our nation.

Below are some of our results and the approximate cost to the Anytown Citizens of this achievement.

Results and Cost

Area	National Average Achievement	Anytown Average Achievement	Our Cost
Reading Achievement	6th	6.6 grade, Our sixth graders are generally six months ahead of the National Average.[4]	$33,160.80
Reading Vocabulary	6th	6.6 grade, Anytown is 6 months ahead of the National Average.	16,580.40
Reading Comprehension	6th	6.9 grade, Anytown is 9 months ahead of the National Average.	16,580.40
Language Mechanics	6th	6.7 grade, Anytown is 7 months ahead of the National Average	33,160.80
Arithmetic Concepts	6th	6.8 grade, Anytown is 8 months ahead of the National Average.	13,264.32
Arithmetic Application	6th	6.9 grade, Anytown is 9 months ahead of the National Average.	13,264.32

> Photographs of testing and Library facilities

---

[4] In 1968 these same students were one month below the third grade National Average.

A COMPARISON OF STUDENT ACHIEVEMENT

AND RELATED COSTS!

Kindergarten Achievement/Cost Statement Based Upon the Psychologist's Report on Kindergarten Achievement, May, 19--.

Test Instrument Used

Metropolitan Reading Readiness Test - Kindergarten Level Test, Based Upon 12,225 Kindergarten Age Students, Nationwide Reliability Determined to be 85% - Copyright Date, 19--.

School	National Average Score	Anytown 19-- Average Score	Number of Months Our Students are Ahead of the Nat. Average Reading Readiness
South	55	56	One month
Central	55	63	Eight months
Peach	55	60	Five months
Apple	55	62	Seven months
East	55	62	Seven months
June	55	61	Six months
April	55	68	One year
North	55	63	Eight months
West	55	55	at National Level

School	Our Cost	Number of Teachers [5]	Number of Students	Per Pupil Cost
South	$ 8,639.42	½	34	$254.10
Central	6,615.76	½	32	206.75
Peach	13,166.24	1	42	313.49
Apple	11,731.59	1	61	192.33
East	12,001.49	1	62	193.58
June	12,273.43	1	52	236.03
April	14,864.43	1	48	309.68
North	7,382.58	½	33	223.72
West	12,422.05	1	42	295.76
	$99,096.99 [5]	7½	406	

```
┌─────────────────────────────────────────────────────────────┐
│                                                               │
│        Photographs of Elementary Reading Program              │
│                                                               │
└─────────────────────────────────────────────────────────────┘
```

---

[5]Teachers with more experience and more educational preparation are paid higher salaries, thus the resulting cost difference.

ANYTOWN ELEMENTARY SCHOOL
COSTS PER SQUARE FOOT

Square footage area as determined by AIA Document D-101 - 21,800 sq. ft.

	Amount	Cost per sq. ft.
General Trades (Base Bid)	$238,000.00	$10.87
Plumbing (Base Bid)	54,786.00	2.50
Heating & Vent. (Base Bid)	91,595.00	4.18
Electrical (Base Bid)	43,550.00	1.99
	$427,931.00	$19.54
Office Addn. (Alt. B-1) (1,490 sq. ft.)		
General Trades	$ 12,500.00	$ 8.38
Heating & Vent.	2,487.00	1.66
Electrical	3,170.00	2.12
	$ 18,157.00	$12.16
Building including B-1	$446,088.00	$19.08

The funds used to print and mail this report were donated by the below listed community organizations as a public service.

Photographs of the New Building

DEDICATION PROGRAM

Invocation . . . . • Reverend
                                                  Anytown Community Church

Pledge of Allegiance

Welcome . . . . • Superintendent
                                                  Anytown School District

Introduction of Guest and Board of Education

Presentation of Building . . . . • Architect

Acceptance of Building . . . . • President
                                                  Anytown Board of Education

Thanks and Acceptance . . . . • President
                                                  Anytown Parent Teachers Organization

                                                  Principal
                                                  Anytown Elementary School

                                                  Student Representative

America Our Heritage . . . . • Elementary Chorus Director

Benediction . . . . • Catholic Church Representative

Open House

7

Projecting Educational Priorities with a Financial Base

Head school administrators have long been faced with the problem of developing a representative appropriations document. This problem has manifested itself in the concept of total involvement. Administrators need to involve the total staff in the development of the appropriations document, while at the same time maintaining a logical control over the direction of program development within the school system. Although these two goals are compatible, they are in conflict with regard to staff priorities. In order to compromise this conflict, it is essential that the total staff be involved from the very beginning of the process which develops the appropriations document and the annual budget.

How a Budget Could Be Compiled from the Building Level by Using "CAS"

Once the basic decision to involve staff has been made, it becomes necessary to develop a formal organizational structure which will allow orderly involvement of total staff and school personnel. The CAS System of developing a school appropriations document allows for total involvement and total representation among the various factions composing the school staff. All staff members, professional and non-professional, must be represented by counterparts, and their suggestions must be considered when developing the appropriations document. It is logical to assume that the people most directly related to program development would also be the same people with the best concept of what is needed to implement program growth. Who better knows what is needed in the home economics program than the individual home economics teacher? It is obvious that

116

the coordinator of transportation would understand the needs of the transportation system better than an elementary principal, while at the same time, an elementary principal would understand the development of program within his individual building better than a kindergarten teacher. By using the expertise of the various specialists within the school system, and by delegating a responsibility for representing this expertise to these individuals, it is possible to develop an accurate, and also a useful, planning document for the entire school system. Although the reason and purpose for this document is obvious, the necessary organizational structure is not.

Illus. 7-1 is a workable organizational structure which allows for total involvement among staff in the process of developing financial organization within the district. Notice that this example highlights the public as the base or foundation for fiscal development. At the other end of the continuum, the students representing the public through their parents are the goal for justifying the existence of the school district. In other words, symbolically, the public and the students represent the constituency which supports or refutes the program developed by the school district. For this reason, it is essential that the students be involved in the development of the program, thus carrying their involvement and the knowledge of it back to their homes and parents, and the voting public, which eventually approves or disapproves the functions carried out by the system. This type of public involvement insures that the people implementing the school system will be the people developing plans for its improvement. Thus, the program is sandwiched between the people responsible for financing it and the people responsible for benefiting from it. It should be kept in mind constantly that the channels of communication between students and the public are continuous, allowing a positive, consistent means for educating the public to the objectives and priorities within the school system.

Organization

An organized approach to fiscal responsibility allows a place for every idea and for every concept within the school system to be conveyed to those responsible for making decisions with regard to financial expenditures.

Illus. 7-1 is a systematic approach to developing school district organization for the purpose of financial planning. Notice the administrative council, which is made up of all administrators within the school district. This group acts as a judicial body and functions to limit programs by judging their academic value for students in proportion to their financial cost. These K-12 curriculum committees are composed of teachers who represent various subject matter areas within the school district. For ex-

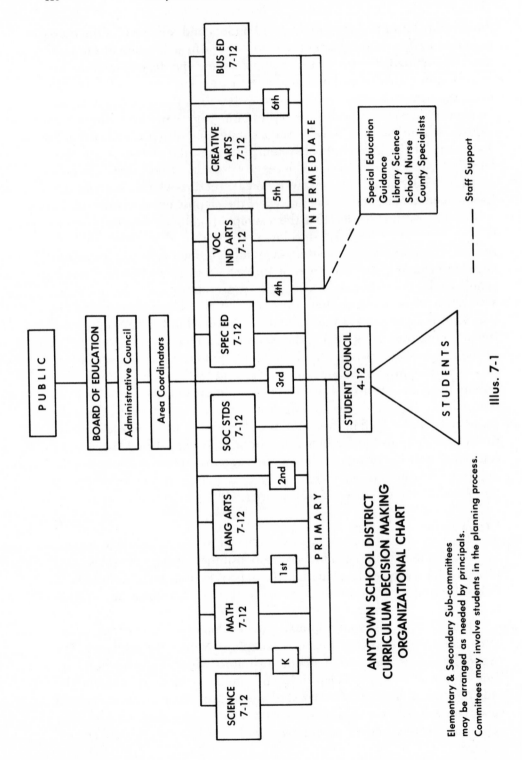

ANYTOWN SCHOOL DISTRICT
CURRICULUM DECISION MAKING
ORGANIZATIONAL CHART

Elementary & Secondary Sub-committees
may be arranged as needed by principals.
Committees may involve students in the planning process.

Illus. 7-1

ample, a K-12 math committee would have teachers which represent each grade level, kindergarten through the twelfth grade, while at the same time these teachers would also represent each building within the school district. It might be that we would have a kindergarten teacher from building A, a first grade teacher from building B, and a second grade teacher from building C, and thus all buildings and all grade levels would be represented by a K-12 math committee. This type of organizational structure allows for ideas to flow freely from the various buildings to the various subject matter committees, while at the same time information from the Board of Education and the administrative council, with regard to financial limitations within the school system, also flows freely toward the building. In this way the buildings are better informed with regard to financial limitations existing within the school system, and staff members suggest more realistic programs with regard to program development. This dual purpose approach to fiscal planning allows for more coherent, realistic proposals from staff participants.

Possibilities During the Second Year of "CAS"

The K-8 grade level curriculum meetings offer some additional benefits with regard to academic program development. A K-8 grade level meeting may be called at any time by any teacher, simply be having that teacher contact her principal and asking for a meeting of all of the other teachers in the school system at that particular grade level. For example, a first grade teacher would approach the principal and say that she would like to meet with all the other first grade teachers within the district. The principal would then send out an announcement that a first grade level meeting would be held during the common planning period of one hour each day allowed each teacher within the system. Once the meeting had been established, the teachers at the first grade level would be responsible for attending the meeting, and bringing along with them any ideas or suggestions with regard to developing the first grade program. This process allows teachers at the same grade level to share ideas and concepts with regard to program implementation at their particular level. At the same time, it involves teachers at one grade level in the common pursuit of program development on a continuous basis. The program which is proposed by the grade level committee is then assigned a dollar value by the administrative council. If the program suggested by the grade level committee does not justify the dollar expenditure as determined by the administrative council, then the program is resubmitted to the committee for reconsideration. If a program suggested by a grade level committee in the area of mathematics is passed on to the K-12 math committee and approved for consideration by the administrative council, then the administrative council would determine if the program had significant value and should be implemented. They would also request that the Board of Education approve the program for the amount of money needed to complete the implementational process. Once this has been done, and the Board of Education approves the program, implementation would commence. Remember, a program that is approved by the Board of Education through this process has involved the teachers at the various grade levels as well as the students, by allowing the students to suggest ideas to the teachers for inclusion in proposed programs. This system involves a K-12 curriculum committee which represents that particular subject matter area, and allows all administrators within the school system to evaluate the student value of the program. This system presents a united front to the Board of Education, including teachers, administrators and students, and if the program is approved by the Board of Education, this united front includes the Board of Education and is presented to the community. This approach insures the public knowledge of the program through its children, who are students involved in its development.

The CAS organizational system also has some additional advantages. Notice the critical issues committee. This committee functions to develop a program in areas which are of current, relevant significance to students. For example, if students need information about drugs, alcohol, sex, tobacco or draft education, this committee would be enjoined to develop a program proposal with regard to implementing a needed program within the school system. The program could consist of a series of lessons or units in the specific area being considered. It could be suggested that this unit be included under one of the traditional headings of the curriculum, such as science or social studies. This unit could be one day, two weeks or six months in length. The committee would be responsible for determining the length of the unit, the subject matter to be covered, and the general subject matter area under which this unit would be implemented. By utilizing this approach to critical issues within the school system, the curriculum remains flexible, yet only grows to the extent needed to satisfy current topics of interest which are needed by students. If an area of the curriculum, such as alcohol or drug education, as time passes, becomes "old hat," then it can be dropped from the curriculum by eliminating the unit which has been temporarily implemented. This allows the curriculum to change and insures flexibility and growth, while, at the same time, it allows a method of eliminating permanent growth so that the curriculum does not become unwieldy and impossible to control. Although Illus. 7-1 shows only one subcommittee, entitled critical issues related to the social studies area, many subcommittees could possibly be developed to handle academic areas of interest within the spectrum of existing academic and vocational curriculum areas.

Area Chairmen

The area chairmen serve a unique yet judicial function within this organizational structure. They are responsible for meeting with departmental committees and developing programs within the high school financial structure. The committee chairmen are responsible for leading the committee in the development of programs, according to limitations imposed by financial restrictions within the school district. These area chairmen are pseudo-administrators. Although they possess no line authority to judge programs, they do possess a knowledge of the circumstances surrounding judgements made by line officers, such as the building principals. This authority is then manifested as information in the process of developing new curriculum areas within the school district. The primary responsibility of the area chairmen lies in the area of complete staff communications. Without this communication link to the departmental committees involving the principal's suggestions, as well as suggestions from the student council, it would be impossible to maintain continuous communication between the administrative structure and the teaching staff. The area chairmen carry the administrative message to the teachers and, while listening to the teachers, convey their concerns to the administration. This communication liason role expedites the development of programs by keeping the components informed of the priorities established by the staff.

Students throughout the school system are included in all of the committees through communication with their representatives and teachers. Teachers are encouraged to seek student opinion concerning new program proposals and old program evaluation. Thus, student ideas are of primary importance in the process of developing new programs. They are involved at all stages within the developmental structure, and can be encouraged to aid in the presentation of programs to the administrative council and Board of Education. This system completes the cycle of involvement which allows all components of the school system to voice an opinion.

In the beginning stages of "CAS," it is essential that a complete formal structure be established. This organizational structure may be informal in its original conception, and later more formalized and regimented. Once the structure has been formalized, faculty and students understand and utilize it more. After a year or two of development, the system becomes a ready and expeditious method of developing programs within the district.

Teachers become more confident that their suggestions will be heard. Students and parents realize that channels are available for curriculum development. All of the constituencies operating within the school district realize that by using the established channels of communication, programs and ideas can be assimilated more expeditiously for all.

Together with the formal organizational structure, other systems need to be developed within the school district to supplement and expedite the gathering of information for the development of financial instruments. Priorities must be established by all groups within the school district. It has been long understood that it is easy to ask for a new piece of equipment or a new program, but more difficult to develop a priority listing of the items most needed. By delegating the responsibility for determining priorities within the school district, bias suggestions for specific areas of specialization within the program are curtailed. It becomes essential for each department and each building staff to determine those things which they consider of highest priority. This obligates them to their various projects and establishes a goal for the staff in implementing their program. If a building staff, for example, decides that a salary increase is more important than new desks for the students, and then six months later makes a request for new desks, it is obvious that the response to their demand should be: "Remember last year's top priority item."

Financial Merit Evaluation

The goal of our accountability system at this point becomes that of developing a complete blueprint for future fiscal spending within the school district. This blueprint, in its final form, will become a catalogue of cost and item priorities for the entire school district. This catalogue will take the form of a notebook with loose leaves for each department, each K-12 curriculum committee, each K-8 grade level committee, and each building within the school district. Both teaching and non-teaching personnel should be involved in developing priorities. As you might expect, there will be some duplication of effort in the process of compiling this blueprint of fiscal spending. However, once the various projects and proposals have been identified, and each building's priorities have been established, the process of eliminating the duplication which is present becomes simple. At the same time, it is possible to compare the priorities of building A with the priorities of buildings C and D and all buildings wtihin the school district. An administrator might discover salary increases are the number one priority for the next fiscal year in building A, while building B might think that the adoption of a new textbook for grade three should be a number one system-wide priority for the next year, and so it goes throughout the buildings within the school district. This information becomes invaluable to a conscientious Board of Education attempting to determine where appropriations should be made for the coming school year. The items which can not be purchased because of financial limitations during the current planning year are carried forward into the next fiscal year, and occupy a higher position of priority. Each group involved in developing the fiscal blueprint for the school district will be allowed to evaluate and adjust its proposal annually.

Group Responsibility

By establishing each group's responsibility for program development within their subject matter area of specialization, program credibility is guaranteed. Once the responsibility for program development has been delegated to each specialized group involved in the formal district organization, they begin to appreciate, understand, and realize the full impact of existing financial limitations within the district. Thus, a side benefit of the system is a better understanding of fiscal limitation within the school district. These curriculum groups also realize that they must implement their program proposals. Thus, human nature dictates that as various groups make program proposals, their involvement insures the implementation of the program and dedication to its accomplishment. If they propose a program, and it is unsuccessful because they are unable to actualize its implementation, this is a discredit to their ability to dictate program development for the school district. Very few teachers are willing to accept responsibility for system-wide development of their subject matter area. For this reason, the logic of the situation is flawless. The people directly responsible for program implementation are also responsible for program development. This dual role of developing program and implementing it insures that maximum effort and dedication will be present after the expenditure is originally approved as a top priority item by the Board of Education. Thus, by delegating the responsibility of spending to teachers, the Board of Education controls the dedication to which teachers will apply themselves to program implementation. This system reinforces the involvement on the part of staff, community and students while it guarantees efficient program development. Once the funds have been appropriated for a new program, teachers from the group who are responsible for its original conception must now be responsible for carrying out the program to its ultimate conclusion. They are also responsible for evaluating and revising their proposals annually and in the final analysis, if the program becomes obsolete, they are responsible for making provision for its eventual elimination.

Total Involvement

This system-wide involvement permeates the entire foundation of an accurate cost accountability system. It forces teachers, students, lay leaders and school administrators to be responsible in making judgements about the program spending. It allows every group within the school system a means of exerting pressure to change its present views with regard to system spending priorities. By accomplishing this, it is possible to eliminate the argument that a group or an individual in a system was not involved in the development of a particular program. Thus, continuity and credibility are insured with regard to futuristic community curriculum development.

Staff Development as a Response to Accountability

School systems all over our nation are presently being challenged with questions concerning accountability in the classroom. Accountability in itself is not the concern. However, accountability becomes the question for which quality education is the solution. It is a well publicized fact that nearly 80 percent of all instructional costs can be attributed to providing staff. With each school district's investment in instructional staff expanding and growing each school year, it becomes increasingly important to develop a procedure for developing the greatest potential from staff members. It is with this purpose in mind that the "CAS" system has established and developed the following procedures for growth and efficiency.

Humanizing "CAS"

The objectives of humanizing "CAS" are direct and simple:

1. To develop individual programs designed for specialized training in areas of need, for teachers and professional staff members.

2. To provide specific instruction on the use and flexibility of system-wide adopted materials.

3. To develop group activities designed for general method and technique improvement.

4. To provide a semiannual in-service evaluation of teacher performance, designed to correct individual difficulties and encourage postgraduate training.

These objectives have long been hallmarks of well developed staff improvement programs; however, the "CAS" approach emphasizes simplicity of purpose, combined with the efficiency of staff improvement.

This system was developed cooperatively through a process involving administrators, teachers, parents, community leaders and students. The purpose of the plan was to originate an organizational pattern for staff fulfillment which would satisfy the needs of all participants, and encourage the growth of quality education for the purpose of satisfying the accountability demanded and expected by a conscientious, progressive community.

Once the organizational goals and ideas for humanizing were established, the stage was set for action. This action came with the formation of an implementation procedure for accomplishing the goals and the objectives of the system.

The same concerns and causes for implementational delay that confront similar programs in education were faced by the "CAS." Hesitancy on the part of the participants, skepticism about program success, and detail involved in organizational development and community direction were phases in the transition from a drawing board project to reality. The "what" to be done had been established, but the "how" was yet to be experienced.

A plan had to be established and individual programs designed for specialized training in all areas of identified needs. Through a process of staff conferences, concerns were identified and individuals were selected for specialized, in-service training programs at the state and national levels, designed to prepare them for instructional leadership in curriculum development. These recognized, dedicated professionals paved the way for staff participation in organizational seminars and workshops designed to provide additional training in academic areas of curriculum. Schedules and timetables evolved during this phase of development. Building level, as well as system-wide kindergarten through twelfth grade concerns, were discussed and staff members at all levels were utilized. Ideas and concepts concerning pre-vocational education, drug education, learning disability programs, achievement assessment, behavioral objective development, differentiated staffing, cluster teaching, as well as several other areas of curriculum development, were discussed. Thus, after identifying, selecting and scheduling teachers and administrators into in-service education programs, designed to meet the individual needs of professional leaders, CAS humanization was developing.

Use of Experts

In retrospect, it was observed that as a result of participation in the various programs and staff development sessions, motivation increased among staff members. Student participation and interest in programs improved, and motivational enthusiasm throughout the school system heightened staff morale to new levels.

In order to provide instruction on the use and flexibility of system wide materials, the following programs were instituted:

Textbook company consultants and material experts were approached to provide the necessary in-service training for teachers, with regard to their specialized material. This approach was both inexpensive in its conception and dynamic in its impact. These people were willing to provide specialized consultant services to the school district. As a result, relationships were improved between the various experts, company representatives and school system personnel.

This constant attention for proper material utilization promoted enthusiasm and increased motivation among classroom teachers and instructors to vary and diversify their utilization of the available instructional materials within the school district. This phase of humanization centered around language arts, including reading, writing and spelling at the elementary levels; math, history, and English at the middle and high school levels; social sciences, biological and physical sciences at the secondary level.

Objective two of "CAS" was successful in reaching the traditional areas of the curriculum and in diversifying the classroom approach to planning for efficient utilization of existing facilities and materials. Objective two of the plan, just as objective one, contributed to the increased conscientious concern for accountability within the instructional program and insured a continued, progressive, quality instructional system for student exposure.

The Humanization Process

Objective three of the humanization process is designed to provide activities for general teaching technique improvement and development. Investigation into resources available for this type of a program proved successful and rewarding. Each college and university contacted, throughout the immediate geographical area, provided a list of skilled and distinguished experts in the various fields of teaching method and instructional technique needed for quality classroom performance. Many authors, teachers, researchers and distinguished scholars were located, manuals were devised, funds were appropriated and timetables were established for making these experts available to the various instructional leaders throughout the school system. Local professionals were contacted, and national educational leaders were approached to become a part of a unified, thorough attack on the problem of increased staff development and growth.

These people were brought into the school system and utilized in diverse ways to involve staff members in discussion groups, reality therapy, recreational brainstorming discussions, individual rap sessions, and other group methods of communication in order to share the vast experiences and philosophies of these professional leaders. These sessions provided a continued resource of new ideas, technical expertise within the classroom, and organizational inspiration for professionals within the school district. Discussions were lively and relevant, based upon immediate concerns, and yielded positive approaches to solving the immediate problems of the teachers involved in the instructional process. The compatability of purpose between professional educators proved to be a unifying factor in the establishment of a continuing, growing rapport between the recognized professional leaders and the teachers within the school district.

All efforts were designed to humanize the instructional process and established a base for continued emphasis upon accountability throughout the "CAS" plan for instructional success.

Objective four of "CAS" involved the semiannual evaluation of instruction staff designed to correct individual difficulties and encourage post-graduate training. A three phase annual evaluation of instructional personnel was utilized. Phase one involved a thorough evaluation of teaching techniques and practices in each classroom situation on an individual basis by each teacher's immediate supervisor. Phase two required a "rap session" between the teacher and immediate supervisor concerning the observations made during the visitation. During this session, sharing between the supervisor and the teacher was of primary concern in the evaluation process. Phase three required a prescriptive approach to the agreed upon concerns of both teacher and supervisor, with regard to observed strengths and weaknesses in the instructional procedure.

The teacher evaluation procedure used to accomplish the fourth objective of humanization involved a detailed teacher evaluation accomplished by three observation periods of approximately twenty minutes, plus an observation of teaching techniques and methods by the building supervisor. For the purpose of this system, the term building supervisor is used in preference to "principal," because of the diversified responsibilities expected from a staff representative not normally associated with the principalship. This program is designed to utilize most efficiently the supervisory capacity of the school system, in an effort to insure quality instruction throughout the educational process.

Co-operation

Phase three of objective four insures that all teachers co-operatively, with their supervisors, will agree upon a prescriptive plan of remedying any instructional deficiency observed. All evaluation programs and procedures in the system are developed in unity with the continuity of the foundational, behavioral objectives of the instructional program within the district.

The following chart represents the organizational structure of the humanization plan.

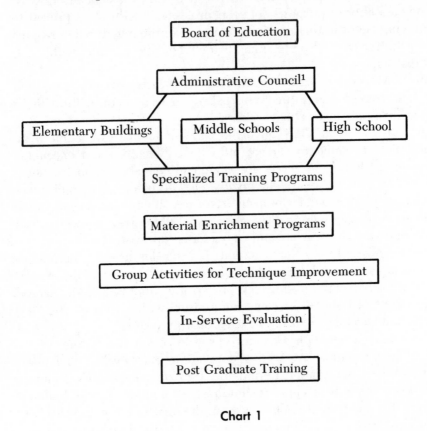

Chart 1

<hr />

[1]The Administrative Council is composed of all administrators employed by the school district. All programs are developed on an individual building basis.

TEACHER EVALUATION SHEET

Last Name	First	Middle		Subject or Grade		Date

School			Appraised by		Position

E - Excellent   S - Satisfactory   N - Needs Help

EVALUATIVE CRITERIA

I   PERSONALITY

___A Neat appearance

___B Works effectively with others

___C Possesses poise and self control

___D Receptive to suggestions

___E Exhibits proper professional attitude

___F Conducive to good parent and
     community relations

II   PREPARATION

___A Makes and uses worthwhile lesson
     plans

___B Participates in professional
     activities

___C Provides for long-range plans

___D Is always prompt and ready for class
     activities

III   TECHNIQUE

___A Exhibits good classroom
     organization

___B Uses variety of materials and
     techniques

___C Provides for student participation

___D Exercises tact and good judgment

___E Possesses knowledge of the total
     growth of children - mental,
     physical, cultural, and social

IV   PUPIL REACTION

___A Pupils seem interested and goal-
     motivated

___B Evidence of educational growth

___C Evidence of development of
     responsibility and self-control

___D Individual differences provided for

___E Maintains proper classroom discipline

SUMMARY OF CONFERENCE

What are the strong points of this teacher?

What are the weaknesses of this teacher?

What suggestions can be made toward helping this teacher grow and improve in areas
where weaknesses are indicated by this evaluation?

Illus. 7-2

EVALUATION SCALE FOR
ADMINISTRATIVE PERSONNEL

CANDIDATE FOR EVALUATION: _____

DIRECTIONS: Please <u>encircle</u> the appropriate number in the scale.

PERFORMANCE SCALE

	Inadequate		Satisfactory		Outstanding

I. EXERCISE OF LEADERSHIP

    A. In total instructional program
       (or special field)

       1. as to knowledge of field(s)   * 5 * 4 * 3 * 2 * 1 *

       2. as to application of knowledge   * 5 * 4 * 3 * 2 * 1 *

    B. In general administration   * 5 * 4 * 3 * 2 * 1 *

II. EXERCISE OF JUDGEMENT

    A. With other people   * 5 * 4 * 3 * 2 * 1 *

    B. With program, plant, etc.   * 5 * 4 * 3 * 2 * 1 *

III. DEALING WITH SPECIAL PROBLEMS AND UNIQUE
     CHARACTERISTICS OF THE JOB RESPONSIBILITY
     (personnel, plant, equipment, etc.)   * 5 * 4 * 3 * 2 * 1 *

IV. PRACTICE OF COOPERATIVENESS WITHIN THE
     SYSTEM AND CONCERN FOR THE GENERAL WELFARE
     OF THE DISTRICT   * 5 * 4 * 3 * 2 * 1 *

 V. SKILL IN THE ACHIEVEMENT OF DESIRABLE PUBLIC RELATIONS

    A. In particular relation to present
       responsibility   * 5 * 4 * 3 * 2 * 1 *

    B. In general on behalf of the entire system   * 5 * 4 * 3 * 2 * 1 *

VI. CONTINUED DEVELOPMENT OF PROFESSIONAL CHARACTERISTICS

    A. By effort made to be alert professionally   * 5 * 4 * 3 * 2 * 1 *

    B. By contributions to the profession   * 5 * 4 * 3 * 2 * 1 *

Evaluation completed by _____   Date _____

Illus. 7-3

QUALITIES OF OVERALL PERFORMANCE

ITEM   EVALUATION (Put x in appropriate box)

		5	4	3	2	1	CE
1. Grasp of Duties	Degree total duties are understood	☐	☐	☐	☐	☐	☐
2. Organizational Skills	Competence in organization	☐	☐	☐	☐	☐	☐
3. Temperament	Mental and emotional maturity	☐	☐	☐	☐	☐	☐
4. Supervisory Ability	Effectiveness in supervision	☐	☐	☐	☐	☐	☐
5. Judgement	Reliance upon facts rather than whims	☐	☐	☐	☐	☐	☐
6. Working With People	Effectiveness in person-to-person relationships	☐	☐	☐	☐	☐	☐
7. Ability to Motivate	Getting the best out of people	☐	☐	☐	☐	☐	☐
8. Accessibility	Making self available to staff	☐	☐	☐	☐	☐	☐
9. Follow Through	Seeing things through	☐	☐	☐	☐	☐	☐
10. Integrity	Consistently carries out promises	☐	☐	☐	☐	☐	☐

Evaluation Code:

        5 Outstanding
        4 Excellent
        3 Satisfactory
        2 Needs Improvement
        1 Very Weak
        CE Can not evaluate; not enough information

Illus. 7-4

ALTERNATE TEACHER EVALUATION FORM

This instrument is designed to serve as a vehicle for a process of cooperative evaluation for growth. It has value only to the extent that it facilitates or serves that process.

Evaluation of the professional staff is so vital to good teaching that a cooperative effort will be made by evaluators at all echelons to hold regular in-service meetings for the purpose of developing the art of evaluation to a qualitatively consistent and high level.

Each of the six major responsibilities has several guides listed. These are not intended to be hard and fast criteria. Rather, they are intended as guides to thinking in considering each responsibility.

Recognizing that the evaluation criteria are not ranked in order of relevancy, it is understood that those to be given the most consideration in evaluating the teacher are the ones which contribute the most to the effectiveness of the teacher in the classroom.

If each teacher will make a sincere effort to evaluate himself in terms of his strengths and weaknesses on each of the six responsibilities listed, and then support that evaluation with an analytical statement, it will surely help to point up areas of strengths and weaknesses. This growth process can be further implemented by a plan of action that will help to shore up weaknesses or amplify strengths.

Each teacher will compare his evaluation and plan of action with one made by his principal. This sharing will be done in a conference held for this purpose. The insights and communication possible with such a process can help to create and maintain an evironment of trust, creativity and mutual respect. In this process this instrument might serve as the catalyst.

NAME _____

SUBJECT AREA _____ DATE _____

_____ Years experience at Anytown _____ Other systems

Type of contract _____ Limited _____ Continuing

Certification _____ Provisional _____ Professional

Illus. 7-5

TECHNIQUES OF INSTRUCTION

Teacher
1. Employs a variety of methods in presenting subject matter.
2. Recognizes and makes provision for individual differences.
3. Stimulates students to greater accomplishment consistent with ability.
4. Inspires confidence in his students.
5. Conducts discussions and group procedures that teach students to express ideas clearly, accurately and completely.
6. Develops understanding of the basic skills, then fixes these skills by meaningful activity.
7. Demonstrates up-to-date knowledge of content and instructional materials in teaching.
8. Keeps abreast of and experiments with new developments in education.
9. Conducts continuous evaluation of the learning program.
10. Displays consistency in handling day-to-day problems of the classroom.
11. Practices and encourages good housekeeping.
12. Recognizes that he teaches what he is as well as what he knows.

I consider my greatest strengths to be:

I consider my greatest weaknesses to be:

My plan to improve in this responsibility is:

High   Satisfactory   Low

/ / / / / / / / / / / / / / /

Illus. 7-6

TEACHER—PUPIL RELATIONSHIPS

Teacher
1. Demonstrates interest in the activities of each student.
2. Is able to develop and maintain a classroom environment that promotes the educational growth of each student.
3. Is able to maintain an empathetic attitude toward students with problems.
4. Maintains respect for each student.
5. Is able to gain the respect of students.
6. Is able to maintain discipline in a consistent, fair and friendly manner without emotional upsets or extremes.
7. Manifestly helps the student to develop a feeling of personal worth and growth.

I consider my greatest strengths to be:

I consider my greatest weaknesses to be:

My plan to improve in this responsibility is:

High   Satisfactory   Low

/ / / / / / / / / / / / / / /

Illus. 7-7

TEACHER—PARENT—COMMUNITY RELATIONSHIPS

Teacher

1. Uses all parent conferences as an aid to better understanding of the child as a means of reporting pupil progress.
2. Encourages parents to contribute to the learning situation of the child.
3. Shows initiative in the improvement of the school-community relations.
4. Encourages the participation of the community resource people in the instructional program whenever such employment contributes substantially to the learning process.

I consider my greatest strengths to be:

I consider my greatest weaknesses to be:

My plan to improve in this responsibility is:

High   Satisfactory   Low

/ / / / / / / / / / / / / / /

Illus. 7-8

TEACHER—PRINCIPAL RELATIONSHIPS

Teacher
1. Welcomes supervisory visits.
2. Supports the accepted school policies.
3. Is receptive to constructive criticism from his principal.
4. Feels free to discuss problems with his principal.
5. Gives constructive criticisms to his principal.

I consider my greatest strengths to be:

I consider my greatest weaknesses to be:

My plan to improve in this·responsibility is:

High   Satisfactory   Low

/ / / / / / / / / / / / / /

Illus. 7-9

TEACHER—STAFF RELATIONSHIPS

Teacher
1. Works closely with total staff for the general welfare of the school.
2. Displays interest in studying problems connected with the instructional program.
3. Assumes responsibility toward new teachers.
4. Accepts assistance from other teachers.
5. Uses available specialized services.

I consider my greatest strengths to be:

I consider my greatest weaknesses to be:

My plan to improve in this responsibility is:

High   Satisfactory   Low

/ / / / / / / / / / / / / /

Illus. 7-10

PROFESSIONAL GROWTH

Teacher
1. Is friendly, neat and courteous.
2. Refrains from discussing problems with those not directly involved.
3. Strives for professional growth by:
        (1) Attending workshops
        (2) Attending summer school
        (3) Attending evening or Saturday classes
        (4) Participating in conferences
        (5) Reading professional books and periodicals
        (6) Participating in community activities
        (7) Traveling and work experience
        (8) Taking an active part in professional organizations

I consider my greatest strengths to be:

I consider my greatest weaknesses to be:

My plan to improve in this responsibility is:

High	Satisfactory	Low

/ / / / / / / / / / / / / /

Illus. 7-11

Selling Educational Priority Adjustment to the Staff and Public

Operating employees must be held responsible for the development of priority proposals in the areas of buildings, cafeteria and transportation systems. The various program coordinators must meet with building principals and develop lists of priorities within their particular buildings. Once again, these priority lists become the foundation for developing a plan for financial expenditures. This plan becomes a long-term fiscal spending blueprint for the school system. These spending patterns are annually adjusted slightly, but generally remain the same. Thus, continuity of purpose is preserved. This continuity allows study and examination of proposed priorities for citizens within the community. Once the community realizes that they can study and examine future spending proposals, they become convinced of system credibility. Thus, the long-term benefit of the program is greater public support among the various pressure constituencies within the school district.

Proposal Summary Sheets

Illus. 8-1 is an example of how a proposal summary sheet could be devised for an elementary building. It would list the source of the proposal, the principal of the building and the custodian. Of course, the subject and the personnel involved should be listed, and additional items relating to cost should also be itemized. A summary sheet of this type could be developed for each school building within the system. The four major areas covered by the classified personnel or operating employees would be buildings and grounds, maintenance, transportation of pupils and cafeteria programs. Once the summary proposal sheet is devised, the Board of Education has a quick, ready reference for the proposals of each building. A table of contents can then be provided to further organize this booklet of total system spending.

PROPOSAL SUMMARY SHEET

Source of Proposal: _____ *Mr. Jones, Principal/Mr. Glass, Custodian* _____

Subject: _____ *Anytown Elementary Buildings and Grounds Priorities* _____

Personnel Involved: _____ *Certificated and Classified Staff* _____

Additional Equipment Needed: _____ *Summer Work Crew. Most* _____

_____ *serious problem is the water leakage at most glass and panel joints.* _____

Total Cost of Proposal: _____ *$11,550.00* _____

Additional Comments: *Repair Items as Listed.* _____

Cost Priority I: _____ *$10,200.00* _____

Cost Priority II: _____ *$ 1,350.00* _____

Cost Priority III: _____ *$11,550.00* _____

Illus. 8-1

Priority Divisions

Illus. 8-2 is a detailed breakdown of priorities as established by Anytown Elementary School. Priority I is listed as repairing windows and panel water leaks at a cost of $10,000.00. Priority II lists repairing plaster at $1,000.00. As you can see, by developing a list of priorities such as this, it is difficult to criticize the Board of Education decision to allocate funds for priority number I, but because there is a lack of funds they are unable to allocate funds for Priority II. Thus, when a report on the annual appropriations document unveils the priority expenditure selections made by the board, criticism is minimized. The Board of Education's credibility for knowing what is needed in the school district and taking steps to fund those projects which are most needed is supported. Administrators develop their roles as listeners while the staff provides program direction. Proposals which are legitimate and needed are recognized and supported by the Administration and the Board of Education. All proposals are documented for future reference and future development. In the following years, proposals will be reevaluated and revised. Thus, a continuous fiscal planning document is developed with long range usage.

ANYTOWN ELEMENTARY SCHOOL
BUILDINGS AND GROUNDS PRIORITIES

Priority I
1. Repair window and panel water leaks[1] $10,000
2. Repair Roof   200

Priority II
1. Repair Plaster   1,000
2. Repair Ceiling in Multi-Purpose Room[1]   250
3. Summer Work Crew—Total Cost District $15,000
   a) Paint 1/3 area in Cafeteria

Maintenance
Done 1. Repair front entry hardware and doors
     2. Repair drinking fountains 1st and 2nd floors

Illus. 8-2

A document of this type becomes an invaluable asset in establishing fiscal credibility within the community. Community leaders are approached and their ideas are shared with the entire staff. Proposals made directly to the superintendent are channeled into the various formal channels of the organization as established by the Board of Education. All proposals are weighed and carefully evaluated. Priorities are assigned to all proposals from sources within the school district, and are established in documented form for future review and revision. A planning document is developed which outlines all the spending priorities of the various constituencies within the school district. This planning document is annually reviewed, revised and reevaluated, and becomes a blueprint for the future growth and development of program and personnel within the district. Annual appropriation documents are developed upon the basis of priorities as established by the specific subject matter experts within the school

---

[1]Cost not yet available; will be given when received.

district. All this information is compiled and organized in a notebook which becomes the base for explaining the complexities of fiscal planning for public school systems. These plans and documents become the foundation for campaigns needed to generate additional funds for the district. This blueprint becomes a goal for the staff, administration, Board, parents and students of the school district. All of these plans and procedures culminate in the development of a structured, organized, formal approach to accountability. The credibility of the Board of Education and administration is enhanced by careful, documented planning implemented by the staff. Agreement becomes acceptable, fashionable fiscal planning. Accountability lends credibility to an established method of program development.

Illus. 8-3 is a personal summary sheet from a high school social studies department. Notice that the subject being proposed is ninth grade social studies. This proposal would involve one additional teacher as well as wall mats and simulation games. The total cost of this proposal has been estimated at $8,000.

PROPOSAL SUMMARY SHEET

Source of Proposal: *High School Social Studies Department*

Subject: *Ninth Grade Social Studies*

Personnel Involved: *1 additional teacher (possible)*

Additional Equipment Needed: *Wall maps, simulation games*

Total Cost of Porposal: *$8,000*

Additional Comments: *The above additional teacher would only*

be needed if this course were required and if this plus the other required

courses increased the length of the school day.

Illus. 8-3

As we study Illus. 8-4, we see the actual scope and sequence which is being proposed for the ninth grade social studies curriculum. This represents a detailed explanation of the program which is being proposed by the social studies department for the high school. The cost of this entire program has been established at $8,000.00. The relationship of this proposal to the total blueprint for instructional spending or the relationship of the

$8,000.00 to the actual appropriations document will be determined by the Board of Education. However, since this is the only proposal made by the social studies department and represents a top priority proposal, its acceptance by the Board is improved. Thus, the importance of the proposal is determined by the group presenting it to the Board and by the merits it contributes, its value to students in the system, and its priority position within a departmental budget. Once again, this structured approach lends itself to developing an attitude of credibility within the system. Involvement is the key word in developing a true accountability, and credibility is the result of that involvement. A structured organizational system designed to make decisions for curriculum development and assign cost priorities to those decisions is essential to maintain a consistent attitude toward proposals and establish credibility within the system.

NINTH GRADE SOCIAL STUDIES

The present scope and sequence of the Social Studies Curriculum is deficient; it lacks a course to integrate the information acquired in earlier social studies classes, and it does not offer an introductory social studies course at the secondary level; thus, a gap lies in our social studies curriculum between the eighth grade and tenth grade.

The Ninth Grade Social Studies course will integrate all previous social science knowledge and will serve to review all previous social studies subjects and open new and broader avenues of interest and understanding.

The major areas of study include the following:
    I. Factors and Facilities of Research
    II. How to Study Problems in Current Affairs and Seek Their Solution
    III. Nature and Importance of Social Groups
    IV. Factors Affecting Social Reactions
    V. Groups and Peers
    VI. The Role of the Family
    VII. Use of Leisure Time
    VIII. Social Institutions
    IX. The Earth and Man
    X. Regions of the World

Illus. 8-4

The general objectives are as follows:
Social Relations
1. To indicate the extreme importance of social relations in human behavior.

2. To describe and interpret the basic characteristics of social groups.
3. To give a well-rounded and balanced view of social life.
4. To develop an objective attitude toward one's own social problems and a concerning and sympathetic attitude toward the problems of others.
5. To give students experience in conducting social research.
6. To give a perspective of cultural growth and change.
7. To indicate the importance of culture in analyzing human social relations.
8. To describe and develop a well-rounded attitude of the various social institutions.

Critical Thinking, Current Events, Civics, and Research
1. To acquaint students with important current affairs.
2. To help students identify important problems and issues, to see how these affect their lives, and to sense what they can do about them.
3. To stimulate a lively and continuing interest in local, state, national, and international affairs.
4. To develop critical and projective thinking.
5. To become better acquainted with newspapers, news magazines, and other sources of information.
6. To encourage students to adopt points-of-view which are free from prejudice and superstitution.

Geography
1. To develop an appreciation and knowledge of the major physical characteristics of the earth.
2. To comprehend the effects of physical geography on population.
3. To locate a student's own geographic position and relate it to the major land masses of the world.
4. To develop a conception of the world as a single family of nations.
5. To improve his skill in interpreting ánd constructing maps and charts.
6. To establish an understanding of how and why the United States and its citizens are involved in and concerned with world affairs.
7. To establish an understanding of how and why the world is becoming more interdependent.
8. To establish the understanding that to a large extent man patterns his living socially, economically, and politically to fit his natural environment by a process of adjustment to changing natural and cultural conditions.

Utilization of Existing System Components

This approach utilizes the components available and existing within all school systems. The present evaluation, budgeting, and organization become essential components of an accountability procedure. This system utilizes the components which are present and readily accessible within the district. It reorganizes a school system as need dictates and develops responsibility within the professional staff for curriculum development. This organizational method guarantees teacher opinion to be heard and students need to be understood. The fact that staff participation and commitment is required insures that implementation will result. The individuals who are responsible for presenting ideas and assigning priorities are also responsible for implementing those ideas and reevaluating priorities. This dual function insures an obligation and commitment to proposals after their original conception. This responsible obligation and commitment of classroom teachers will transfer to the implementational process and insure a natural obligation to success. The procedure costs nothing. The result is a concise, well-structured organizational approach to fiscal spending and curriculum development. The implementational time span required is short, and the results are long-term. Constituencies are satisfied and Board of Education credibility is restored through total involvement. Understanding is maintained between administration and teacher factions within the school district. Communications are improved and Board public appeal is increased as a result of a structured, well-organized plan of disseminating information concerning program development. As the school system gains public support, levies are passed more readily and future programs are developed more completely, which results in better education for boys and girls. A systematic approach to fiscal spending establishes credibility and fiscal accountability.

Delegating Authority

The ultimate value of this system is obvious. By delegating authority for the development of fiscal programs to the individual program specialist, these leaders become responsible for providing financial statements which represent their proposals. This systematic approach to budgeting placed the responsibility for accuracy upon the building staff and administration. Each year the building staff and administration must set priorities with regard to programs, and fund these priorities through their proposals for the appropriations document. Once the appropriations document has been compiled from the bits and pieces of information gathered from each building, the school system is ready to move ahead to the budget document for that year. These proposals may be evaluated and revised by the Board of Education in the normal process of developing the budget. However, in most cases, it is advantageous to accept the proposals as they are made, thus obligating the building staff and administration to the programs which they have suggested. Once again, when this budget is finally approved by the Board of Education, the Board has successfully obligated and encouraged all members of the staff to present their ideas and, in the last analysis, implement their ideas within the school system. This type of sophistication is nearly impossible to achieve during the first year of development. The second year of development allows "CAS" to reach its full influence upon the financial spending within the system. During the second year of operation, approximations become reality. Estimations become fact and the system becomes more accurate and articulate.

Reallocation of Financial Priorities

Another aspect of developing "CAS" is the influence which will be exerted upon the reallocation of financial priorities. Generally, financial priorities are established on a one year basis only. Yet, occasionally it is to the advantage of the system to develop long-range priorities spanning two or three budgeting years. In cases such as this, it is possible that a reallocation of spending could be in order. If this is desired, this reallocation should be made on the basis of financial facts, not opinion. The source of these facts, or the foundation of the fiscal instrument, should be traced back to the group making the original proposal. This approach to reallocation adds credibility to adjustments which must be made in any budget to develop a format which will best serve the district's needs. By establishing cost ratios between each program offered in the district and the number of students served by each program, it is possible to develop a reallocation system which accurately represents objectives established by individual buildings. A system of this type provides documentation supporting reallocation. Thus, as decisions are made to redistribute funds to new programs, evidence of staff desire is obvious.

This highlights the selling points, or justification for the developing of a CAS System. This accountability system has a curricular emphasis, rather than a financial base. It is output oriented and emphasizes activity and programs within the system, evaluating these before implementation. Strategic planning and evaluation of expenditures are also components of an accurate "CAS" procedure. This system reveals values within the community and accomodates public understanding. It provides a systematic analysis for understanding fiscal priorities. A system of this type exhibits a rational, logical, administrative approach to fiscal understanding and becomes a simplifier for budget concepts.

System Selling Points

A conventional budget has financial emphasis and is basically input oriented. It emphasizes objects such as school buses and buildings rather than curriculum. The conventional approach lends itself to an after the fact analysis of fiscal spending, rather than the complete planning concept. The conventional budget attacks technical planning, rather than strategic planning designed to meet student needs. At best, a typical budget monitors expenditures. Traditional budgeting procedures camouflage values within the school system, rather than reveal costs to the community the system serves. Most budgets are established to accomodate accountants and accounting procedures, rather than facilitate better public understanding of fiscal policies. In general, a well established, well organized accounting procedure, which is program oriented, develops a logical approach to administration, rather than a crises management approach. It becomes a simplifier of the complicated financial turmoil which is present in most systems.

Financial Justification of Existing Program Priorities

Financial justification of existing program priorities is of critical importance to school planners. A cost accountability system provides decision makers with accurate data for planning programs and executing policies. It spells out explicitly the objectives of school program priorities. CAS systematically analyzes alternative methods of achieving program objectives in an effective and efficient manner. Total cost estimates, rather than partial approximations, can be achieved. Programs may be reviewed and evaluated on a continuing basis, instead of being placed hastily on a schedule which is designed to accomodate only accountants. Attention may be focused upon future educational environments and pending growth projects within the school system. The basic management information system provided by CAS will allow one to analyze his mode of approaching problems and better establish planning calendars and budgeting cycles. Faculty, students and community alike are encouraged to participate in the planning process and provide additional information for decision making within the system.

The major purpose of a management information service is to provide the basis for justifying existing program priorities in the system. Typical budgets develop little program accountability. Procedures normally are nonexistent for the establishment of program priorities. Financial requests unrelated to fiscal taxing power are difficult to accommodate within existing funds. Expenditures are not properly identified with specific programs, and become targets for constituency pressure groups disenchanted with the system. There is an absence of measurement, evaluation and student achievement testing within the system. Time and again, administrative authority overrules administrative responsibility, and poor decisions result, hindering the educational process. If alternatives are not analyzed systematically, the result is poor planning and weak implementation.

Community Involvement

Today, school systems are constantly plagued by community involvement. A well organized CAS approach to management information allows committees to be formed which become responsible for maintaining continuous communications with these factions. Some typical committee designations are long-range planning, curriculum priorities, student development, program evaluation and economic resource. Once the committees begin to function, documents which generate public support must be prepared for community distribution. These could take the form of program budget presentations or program accomplishment reports, or explanations of new program proposals. Meetings should be held to discuss questions concerning new programs being developed within the school district. At these meetings, the following questions should be asked: What new programs should the schools offer? Which existing programs should be given priority? What educational time allocation and funding should be given to the reading program? How can the schools provide leisure time programs for adults? Answers to these and other questions become the highlights of committee discussion. This involvement insures community participation in school planning, and allows administrative functions to surface during the process of system redesign.

A CAS System structures the program and its objectives, and develops its description. It establishes a budgetary document which can be maintained and updated yearly. It produces a financial record of planning and development internally, which insures close fiscal control. Memoranda and procedural directives are supplied through this management information system. The budget cycle and planning timetable are syncronized to allow for a more complete cost accounting and coding structure. Curriculum taxonomy objectives are prevalent and document the fiscal planning which has taken place. Performance indicators, such as standardized testing, add credibility to the evaluation criteria as it is applied to the system. Capital facilities are surveyed, evaluated and distributed according to a programmed approach. This system lends itself to automation, and can easily be transformed into data banks for computer documentation. A simulation model of the CAS System can contribute to the improvement of the decision making process and organize the repetitive functions of the operation. All of these factors culminate in the efficient time utilization of staff and administration.

Humanizing "CAS"

Since all school systems are made up of programs, and programs are composed of people, an accurate cost accountability system is cognizant of the value of people. A cost accountant would refer to CAS as a time study in education. The most valuable asset which the teacher brings to the classroom is time. A careful study of that time and the utilization of it is a prerequisite to an efficient cost accountability system. Without documented records and precise planning concerning both educational objectives and evaluation of achievement, it is impossible to develop a precise calculation of time utilization applied to program implementation.

"CAS" PROGRAM REDUCTION

Approximate Cost of Proposed Program Reduction at the
Anytown Senior High, both Jr. Highs and all Elementary Buildings

Course	No. of Sections	Approximate Cost of Program
Animal Science	1	$3,287.16
Agronomy	1	3,287.16
Ag. Engineering	1	3,287.16
Farm Mech.	1	3,287.16
Farm Business Analysis	1	3,287.16
Art III	1	5,224.03
Art IV	1	5,224.03
Bookkeeping II	1	2,927.72
BOE (Jr.)	1 x 5 Periods	13,300.43
Business Principles	1	3,144.45
Record Keeping	1	2,927.72
Shorthand I	1	2,927.72
Shakespeare	1	4,220.65
Drama	2	9,008.52
Novel	1	4,220.65
Speech I	1	4,220.65
Speech II	1	4,220.65
Expository Writing	1	4,220.65
Journalism	1	4,220.65
French III	1	4,231.35
French IV	1	4,231.35
Home Economics III	1	4,737.13
Home Economics IV	1	4,737.13
Foods	1	4,737.13
Clothing	1	4,737.13
Home & Int. Dec.	1	2,373.57 Sem.
Child Care	1	2,373.57 Sem.
Math Seminar	1	4,864.87
Music Appreciation I	1	4,189.81
Music Appreciation II	1	4,189.81
Cost of Program Reduction at H. S.		$131,847.17
Cost of Shorten Sr. H. Sch. Day		47,859.20
Total Cost Program Reduction at H. S.		$179,706.37

Phy. Ed. & Health back to back ½ sem. each
Average number High School Sections per day 42.

Illus. 8-5

Jr. High Proposed Reductions

At the Jr. High level the proposed reductions will occur at the section level rather than the course level.

Courses to Be Affected by Section Reduction	Approximate Cost of Section Reduction
1. Language Arts (Reading)	$42,120.11
2. Art	12,034.32
3. Home Economics	12,034.32
4. Industrial Arts	12,034.32
5. Music	12,034.32
6. Physical Education	12,034.32
7. 6th Grade	18,051.48
	$120,343.19
Cost of School Day Reduction	36,242.35
Total Cost of Jr. High Program Reduction	156,585.54

Activity period cost is included in cost of school day reduction.

Elementary Proposed Reductions

Sections Reduced	Approximate Cost of Section Reduction
1st Grade	$17,191.88
2nd Grade	17,191.88
3rd Grade	17,191.88
4th Grade	17,191.88
5th Grade	17,191.88
Total Cost of Elem. Section Reduction	$85,959.40
Cost of School Day Reduction	36,242.35
Total Cost Elementary Program Reduction	$122,201.75

Illus. 8-5 (Con't.)

Obviously, without such documented, detailed, and evaluative reports of staff utilization and student exposure, it is impossible to develop credibility among the diverse constituencies which challenge the educational process as ineffective and inefficient. However, by comparing time applied to the educational process with achievement derived from the educational process, the picture is complete, and the price and the product are comparable in units of time which helps the conscientious school administrator develop a credible program strategy. These factors highlight the intrinsic value of developing a sophisticated approach to public understanding.

"CAS" TEACHER SALARY NEGOTIATIONS INPUT

As you know, the Teachers Association is still holding out for more money. The Board of Education, with your support, is continuing to fight against the excessive demands of the teacher organization leaders.

I hope the following information will help you to continue to support our Board of Education. Our teachers have received the following salary increases since 19-- :

Year	Base Increase	Average Yearly Increment	Average Insurance Increase	Total Average Yearly Increase
67-68	200	180	None	$ 380
68-69	350	256	162	768
69-70	325	272	173	770
70-71	300	286	178	764
71-72	325	300	186	811
72-7-	300	325	239	864

Amount each teacher has received in increases since 19-- -------- $4,357.

Illus. 8-6

Teachers Retirement: This is the amount of money paid monthly out of a teacher's pay check into the State Retirement System, however, every cent deducted from a teacher's pay check must be matched by the Board of Education. Thus, as the rate of deduction increases, all teachers receive an automatic increase in money received. In 19-- the rate was 11.5% - now it is 12.9% and soon it will be 15%. This is additional money each teacher receives automatically when hired into the system.

On December 21, 19--, I met with the teachers negotiation team and we discussed the following increases:

1. **Present salary base - $7,000.**   2. **Present insurance - $240.**

		Base Salary Increase	Insurance Increase
1.	Effective 1-1-73	$7,450 plus increment	$120 per year to $360
2.	Effective 1-1-74	7,650 " "	Same " " " $360
3.	Effective 1-1-75	7,850 " "	$120 " " " $480
4.	Effective 7-1-7-	8,000 " "	Same " " " $480

This would mean that next year a teacher who is presently making $13,615 would be making $14,450, or an increase of $835 for 180 days work.

$14,450 + 180 days = $80.00 per day

Our administrators work 250 days per year.

A Principal's salary is $15,645 x 250 days = $62.00 per day

A Superintendent's salary is $20,000 x 250 days = $80.00 per day

I do not believe an additional year's experience always makes a better teacher. There are good first-year teachers.

The teachers organization refused the above proposal. They are asking for much more than we can afford to pay without absolutely draining our budget, which can only lead to more taxes.

I give you this information so that you may form your own opinion. I hope that you continue to support your Board of Education. Tell them how you feel - that's the only way they will know!

This memo could be sent by a Superintendent of Schools or a Board of Education President.

Illus. 8-6 (Con't.)

EXAMPLES OF COURSE DESCRIPTIONS WITH "CAS"

Speech II

Prerequisite: Speech I

1/2 Credit

Description: Speech II is a course
for students who have interest in
interpretation and dramatics or debate.
Although most of the class time is spent
on dramatics, students interested in
debate are allowed to work in independent
study.

General Objectives: To encourage
students to become "theater goers,"
to appreciate the planning and work
that goes into a dramatic production by
producing a play themselves, and to
encourage students to participate in
college and/or community theater.

Journalism I

Prerequisite: Junior

1/2 Credit

Journalism I is a survey course
stressing fundamentals of newspaper
work. The course is a prerequisite
for students becoming members of
The Forum and Jacket Journal staffs.

Journalism II

Prerequisite: Journalism I

1/2 Credit - This credit may not be
considered towards fulfilling the
3-English-credit requirement for
graduation.

Journalism II is a continuance of newspaper training with emphasis on the
preparation of the student newspaper.

Expository Writing

Prerequisite: Junior

1/2 Credit

This is a skill course: "how to" develop
your own ideas in clear writing; "how to"
explain, analyze, and report in an
orderly process; "how to" respond to
essay test questions and theme paper
assignments. This is not a creative
writing course.

Contemporary Readings

Prerequisite: Junior

1/2 Credit

This course attempts to explore and
evaluate current American thought through
poetry, essays, the short story, and
current events, including the emerging
Black American culture from its African
roots to its role in modern America.

Students should have skill in reading. This
course is a good choice for students planning
to attend the JVS their senior year.

Communication Media

Prerequisite: Junior

1/2 Credit

Description: Communication Media is an
effort to respond to the facts and judgments
of our advancing electrical technology.
It sets out an inquiry/discovery program
aimed at helping people to understand,
analyze, evaluate, and judge the experiences
they have had and how they are affected by
our communication media.

General Objectives: The general course
objective is to make the student aware of
the impact of mass media, how it affects his
life, and how he can utilize it. It also
gives the student a first-hand understanding
of just what it takes to use media well.
Students should have skill in reading. This
course is a good choice for students planning
to attend the JVS their senior year.

Illus. 8-7

9

Staff and Public Involvement in Developing CAS

A recurring theme of this book has been the production and use of more understandable and meaningful curricular, financial and evaluative information. The process is effective in producing results for a school staff, and is equally effective in involving and reporting to the public in general, who are demanding a forthright accounting of educational expenditures. To answer the demand for accountability, which really means the public trust and credibility for educational institutions, CAS has the unique advantage of being able to explain both strengths and shortcomings of the educational enterprise.

Confronted with spiraling costs of public and private education, taxpayer resistance throughout the country has heightened to levels unprecedented in the history of American public education. In such a climate, levies and budgets face rough treatment.

When they are defeated, an atmosphere of hostility, negativism and suspicion between schools and the public arises. Many acrimonious statements are made, morale is affected, and the administration and the Board of Education work under severe restrictions to rework budgets, and find that, generally, no matter what adjustments are made, some pressure group will demand that some other part of the budget should be cut.

The very public that flayed the Board and administration in the first place for the original size of the budget will endlessly oppose every reduction in its own pet area of interest. Teachers will defend especially those programs that provide summer and supplemental income. Students will present petitions regarding extra-curricular activities or certain favored courses. In general, all groups will want more services at lower cost, and smaller classes with less taxes.

Foresight, not Hindsight

From the beginning, CAS will help in such difficult situations. For example, Illus. 9-1 and 9-2 show a beginning stage of CAS analysis that relates both certified and noncertified staff to various functions in the district. Armed with a beginning Level I to Level II breakdown of the budget and other elementary information shown in Illus. 9-3, the board and administration have a factual analysis at hand, and the staff and public have some rational basis upon which to judge proposals for cuts or reallocations.

CERTIFIED PERSONNEL
STAFFING CHART

	Classroom	Kdg.	Reading	Library	Spec. Ed.	Counseling	Art Music Phys. Ed.
Elementary							
Arlington	20	2	1	1			2.1
Baird	20	2	1	1			2.4
Central	8	0	.5	.5			1.2
Farrow	16	1.5	1	1	3		2.1
Fisher	18	2.5	1	1			2.1
Gensimer	16	1	1	1		.5	1.8
George	2	0					.6
Isaacs	17	2	1	1	1–help		1.8
Mentor	16.5	2.5	1	1	1–help		1.8
Sunderland	15	1	1	1			1.5
Sylvan	10	1	.5	.5		.5	1.2
Tarrow	9	1	.5	.5			.9
Taylor	0	2					
Total = 230.5	167.5	18.5	9.5	9.5	5	1.0	19.5
Middle School							
East	24		1	1		1	
North	30.5		1	1		1	
West	27		1	1	2	1	
South	25.5		1	1		1	
Total = 121	107		4	4	2	4	
High School							
Lincoln Washington	146.5		3	4	2	9	
Total = 164.5	146.5		3	4	2	9	

Illus. 9-1

	Classroom	Kdg.	Reading	Library	Spec. Ed.	Counseling	Art Music Phys. Ed.
P.P.S.							
Pupil Pers. Serv. 11							
TOTALS 527=	432	18.5	16.5	17.5	9	14	19.5

Illus. 9-1 (Con't.)

NONCERTIFIED PERSONNEL
STAFFING CHART

	Secretaries	Custodians	Cooks	Teacher Aides	Lib. Aides	Cross. Gds.	Bus. Drivers	Mechanics	Nurses	Bookkeepers Office Managers	Lunchroom Supv.	Bus Loading Supv.	Playground Supv.	Co-op
Elementary														
Arlington	1	4	2	.5	1	2					1	1	1	
Baird	1	4	3	2	1	2					1	1	1	
Central	1	3.1	1.5	1	1						1	1	2	
Farrow	1	4	2	2	1	1					1	1	2	
Fisher	1	4	3	1	1	1					1	1		
Gensimer	1	3.5	2		1	1					2	1	2	
George												5		
Isaacs	1	4	3	1	1						1	1	2	
Mentor	1	3.5	2	.5	1	2					1	1	2	
Sunderland	1	3.5	2	1	1	3					1		1	
Sylvan	1	3	1.5	.5	.5	3					1	.25	.25	
Tarrow	1	2.5	1.5	.5	.5	1					1	1	1	
Taylor						1								
Total	11	39.1	23.5	12	10	17					12	14.25	14.25	
Middle School														
East	3	9	3	2										
North	3	9	5	3							1			
West	3	9	5	4										
South	3	8.9	4.5	2	1						1		2	
Total	12	35.9	23.5	11	1						2		2·	
High School														
Lincoln	10	22	10	8	2									6
Washington	·6	18	6	4	2									3
Total	16	40	16	12	4									9
Central Office	15.6	5								2				1
Transportation	1						48	3						
Adult Education	1													
Detached	1													
Pupil Pers. Serv.	2								3					
GRAND TOTAL	59.6	120	57	35	15	17	48	3	3	2	14	14.25	10	
												16.25		

Illus. 9-2

RANK ORDER OF PROGRAMS

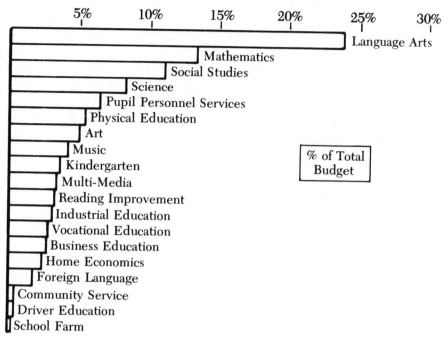

FUNCTION-OBJECT		PROGRAM	% OF TOTAL	AMOUNT BUDGETED
Instruction	$9,353,200	Art	5.0	652,600.00
Administration	420,800	Business Education	2.6	331,500.00
Health and Nursing	36,700	Community Service	.2	24,700.00
Transportation	374,700	Driver Education	.2	20,800.00
Operation	1,489,500	Foreign Language	1.6	209,300.00
Maintenance	405,000	Home Economics	2.3	295,100.00
Fixed Charges	681,500	Industrial Education	3.0	393,900.00
Capital Outlay	84,100	Kindergarten	3.5	455,000.00
Community Services	26,000	Language Arts	23.9	3,108,300.00
Student Services	6,000	Mathematics	13.3	1,723,800.00
Athletics	120,000	Multi-Media	3.3	430,300,000
Outgoing Transfers		Music	4.2	544,700.00
Tuition	2,500	Physical Education	5.3	685,100.00
		Pupil Personnel Services	6.4	835,900.00
		Reading Improvement	3.2	418,600.00
		School Farm	.1	15,600.00
		Science	8.3	1,072,500.00
		Social Studies	11.0	1,426,100.00
		Vocational Education	2.7	356,200.00

Illus. 9-3

CAS was devised as an answer to problems before the crisis, rather than after the fact. When fully developed, it is capable of answering three major, critical requirements that must be met in order to provide better information and relations with the public and others concerned with education:

1. Greater community involvement in the budget process.
2. Better explanation of the services to be provided by tax dollars.
3. Relevant information for decision making on the budget.

CAS meets these general requirements because of the following reasons:

1. Information about specific subject areas and special services is organized and presented in an understandable manner.

2. The objectives of programs are clearly identified.

3. The staff, in setting priorities, considers the entire program, K-12. They also consider the relationship between subject areas, which results in the allocation of resources in line with the agreed upon district-wide priorities.

4. The services received and provided for the taxpayers are related to specific dollar amounts. CAS attempts to integrate the financial plan fully with the educational program, so that the community obtains a comprehensive view.

5. Information provided allows for identification of specific services which would be curtailed or lost as a result of reductions in the budget. The public is generally unwilling to support most reductions once they recognize the specific services to be reduced.

6. The integration of the fiscal plan with the educational programs allows the Board and the administration to go to the taxpayers with a budget that they feel is educationally defensible, as well as financially responsible.

Pitfalls of Reporting

One should not get the idea that CAS is a panacea and that there are no pitfalls to be avoided. These pitfalls arise around two general areas:

1. Communication between the Board, administration, staff, community and students.

2. The evaluative process, which generally centers around the release of standardized test scores related to dollar amounts.

The communication problems soon surface and cause trouble when the Board and administration are unaware of the communication requirement of CAS, or choose to ignore the problem.

Also there seems to be a widespread misconception that the CAS process is merely some new bookkeeping system, and the accountability assignment in countless districts is dumped into the lap of the school business official, who, generally, has never had public relations or system-wide communication as his major function before.

It soon is apparent that CAS, in reality, is a management, planning and evaluation procedure which calls for more public and staff involvement and planned communication than school districts ordinarily use in education program development.

The communication test begins with the setting of educational goals and objectives, in terms which can be evaluated and which are understood and agreed to by the community and the staff. Few school systems have any sort of system for methodically moving through curricular changes, and when the curricular change is also tied to financing, it further compounds the problem.

Using CAS, financial and manpower resources are budgeted for the programs decided upon to achieve these objectives. This, too, is a manner of thinking which very few school districts have indulged in. It is one thing to think of functions such as administration, transportation, and instruction; but it is another thing to think in terms of a language area program which subsumes the cost of transportation, administration, instruction, etc. within the program itself.

The final step in CAS of evaluating the progress made, and relating this to dollar costs as well as the extent to which educational objectives and goals have been met, also adds another dimension to communication problems.

Providing Staff and Community Involvement Through CAS

The business of getting staff and community involvement at this level of CAS development requires many months of careful planning and communication action. All school employees, as far as possible, should be gradually involved in briefing and study sessions. This is not to say, of course, that central office personnel, in the meantime, cannot be working to gather information which will make their management of the school system more effective.

Communication in CAS, or any endeavor with which the school is operating, requires that the job be done slowly and correctly the first time with a solid foundation provided for all concerned. If not, the job will have to be done anyway, and the second effort will be very difficult to achieve because of the distrust caused by the initial failure.

If broad based public participation in the decision making process is an objective, preparation should be made to invest a substantial amount of staff effort to communication know-how. This has been the experience of those who have engaged in CAS development.

In one large city, for example, the school Board, administration and the PTA were engaged for weeks in the initial phase of their study designed to involve maximum community participation and a study of education needs. The PTA, seeking to obtain citizen views on educational issues, used telephone interviews, house-to-house calls, booths in public places, suggestion boxes, coffee hours, student opinion surveys and discussions, bake sales and dinners as vehicles for obtaining information. Next, a formal community attitude study was conducted, and the advance work by the PTA used as a basis for the questionnaire. Illus. 9-4 reproduces five of the thirteen goals which emerge, and displays their unique presentation format and summary analysis by importance and achievement, as perceived by all members of the school community.

After study, the Board used the results to determine future programs and financial plans based upon CAS analysis, which Illus. 9-4 indicates is the second most important goal for the district. The project was simple in philosophy, but produced excellent involvement and results.

State Boards Get Into the Act

A State Board of Education began to prepare their recommendations two years prior to their presentation to the state legislature. The process began with a statewide opinion poll to learn about citizen education concerns and views on educational priorities. A list of priority objectives was developed, and is now systematically reviewed on a regular basis.

Another unique approach in a different state was a series of fourteen regional meetings held by the State Board. Those town meetings attracted the participation of many thousands of citizens who were invited to participate in a free and wide ranging discussion of educational issues. The State Board substantially revised its own list of priorities as a result of the information obtained.

The next step was to develop a position paper for priority items giving means for solving the problem, proposed accomplishments, and alternate procedures. After approval by the Board, the various priorities were put together in a CAS proposal for the state legislative consideration. If there was one single, lasting conviction that the people received from these meetings, it was that a free and open dialogue must be maintained between citizens and individuals in a position of policy making or administrative responsibility.

Shared Leadership

Leaders in a school district in Ohio decided positive action was

ANALYSIS OF SURVEY RESULTS

GOAL

1. Developing Respect for Self and Others
    Anytown education must assure the
    development of youth to have self–respect,
    respect for others and good citizenship.

2. Providing for Efficient Spending
    Anytown education must provide a quality
    educational program by obtaining the
    most value for each tax dollar.

3. Developing the 3R Skills
    Anytown education must provide for the
    learning of basic communication and math
    skills to the fullest extent possible for
    each student.

4. Preparing for a Career
    Anytown education must provide each
    individual the opportunity to select and
    prepare for a career.

5. Providing for the Talented & Handicapped
    Anytown education must provide for
    special educational needs of those who are
    academically talented and those who are
    handicapped.

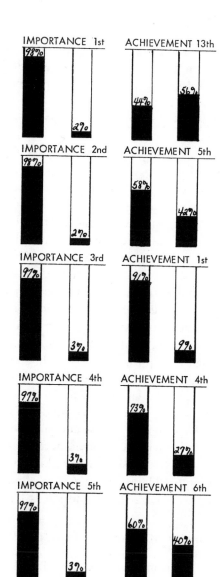

Illus. 9-4

needed to help close the school communication gap which resulted after
levy defeats, strikes, sanctions and court injunctions. The Board, adminis-

tration and education association wisely sponsored a forty member coalition for education of various community organizations. It now holds meetings for an interchange of community and school information and community opinion feedback. The three member steering committee of citizens plans the program and provides a two-way street for such discussions. This community is also very active in developing a cost accountability system as an integral part of the total process.

Sharing Test Results

Probably the most sensitive CAS area centers around the reporting of pupil progress. Ten years ago, school administrators and others in education were strongly opposed to national assessment. Today, however, a growing number of school officials are not only thinking seriously about releasing scores for the district, but are actually doing it. Some even release results in a way once considered more inflammatory than any other, that is by individual schools, rather than by the district. The reason, of course, is to satisfy mounting public desires and demands for accountability and hard data on what schools are accomplishing with public money.

This is the same reason why state legislatures and state education departments have begun to require public test results annually. California introduced public reporting of results in 1965, and in 1969 extended the release requirement through grade twelve. The states of Michigan and Virginia are also currently involved in this process.

Several large school districts, including Tulsa, Oklahoma and Columbus, Ohio; medium size school districts, such as New Rochelle, New York and Springfield, Ohio; and smaller school districts, such as Mount Vernon, Ohio have been involved in the release of such information over a period of several years. More will be involved as the legislative and public pressure mounts. They recognize, as others will, that such public release of test scores is hazardous unless it is handled in a propitious manner.

Dangers of Releasing Test Scores

Foremost among possible dangers in releasing test scores is public misunderstanding. The grade equivalence scores most commonly used to express achievement tend to be uppermost in the mind of the typical taxpayer or newspaper reporter, and explanations, generally, are dry or do not adequately explain the factors that should be considered with such scores. For example, in many school districts there are different programs, socio-economic levels and other factors in different buildings, and there is real danger when the community starts comparing schools or grades by average test standings. Illus. 9-5 delineates some of these factors.

SCHOOL DISTRICT HUMAN AND FINANCIAL INFORMATION

Professional instructional staff per 1000 students
Teachers per 1000 students
Average years teaching experience
Percent of teachers with MA degree and above
Average contracted teacher salary
Percent minority
Percent racial-ethnic minority of students
Grade membership
Total membership

Illus. 9-5

Teachers in the low scoring schools especially feel that they are on the firing line. It is difficult enough for professionals to use the results with necessary insight, even when the report cautions them to be careful not to use the results in isolation when comparing either teachers or youngsters. Also, test results rarely reflect more than the work of the schools in the cognitive domain, neglecting completely the psycho-motor and affective domain.

In essence, release of such information should tell everything or it should not be released. Accordingly, soon after the release of test results, provisions should be made to hold open discussions, to meet with the public to generally explain tests and test scores, to discuss differences in the results due to widely differing pupil expenditures and other factors, and to give recommendatinos for district action in areas where the schools appear weak.

Prior to announcing results, the School Board should issue background news statements and hold informal press briefings explaining how to interpret test results. With advance preparation, no special difficulties develop.

Announcing Test Results

Out of experience, when such test results are to be announced, these points should be kept in mind:

1. Ideally, results should be reported by progress over a period of years.

2. The need for special evaluation of innovative programs should be explained.

3. The test results should be accompanied by a statement of what the results mean.

4. School by school results should be reported on related factors whenever possible.

5. Avoid implying that national norms are desirable standards.

6. Avoid using grade equivalent scores, if possible.

7. Reports should not be limited to medians.

8. Composite scores for each school invite misinterpretation and misuse.

9. Consider ways to separate scores for special samples.

10. Prepare a comprehensive summary of test results for the local press.

11. Introduce the results with a basic explanation.

12. Don't release the report to the public unless the public is prepared.

If the scores are low in the school district, the following course of action can be taken.

1. Explain what national norms are, what they do and what they do not mean.

2. If test results are low compared to national norms, but better than those of previous years, this should be stated, since it indicates improvement.

3. Outline new programs that would be needed to improve performance in specific grades or schools, and outline plans for such which have been made.

4. Report on special or national norms that match grades or schools in the district more closely than general national norms.

5. Stress and document important learning outcomes not measured by standardized tests, such as in the areas of physical education, music, health, etc.

6. Develop, and communicate with test results, other long-range measures of school system accomplishment, such as students' graduate occupations and starting salaries, or the percentage of students going to college.

Teaching Staff Involvement

Another pitfall which should receive attention is the teachers' and the teacher association's attitude toward accountability. A good summation of this attitude might be that teachers do not object to being held accountable if they have had an opportunity to participate in devising and developing an accountability system, and if they have received logistic and administrative support for the school program. In most districts, teachers feel they need pre- and post-certification training for skills needed in new curricular adoption. Generally, teachers feel they are not getting such training either from the colleges or in-service programs of the school systems themselves. Additionally, teachers feel that administrators have not been adequate in their management skills, and are, in essence, blaming the teachers for their own mistakes. They feel that teachers are victims of problems created by society itself. They argue that if accountability measures are used, then the engines that furnish the energy to develop the objectives for feedback mechanism which are used to prove quality and relevance in education should involve them. All such negative reaction can be eliminated by a gradual application of CAS and increasing involvement of teachers. Appendix O details a specific plan for developing a systems approach to curriculum change involving administration, teachers, students and the public in varying stages.

It becomes apparent, however, that regardless of the problems, public relations pitfalls, and problems that may be encountered, as school dollars become increasingly scarce, educators are going to be compelled to develop systems approaches to learning. This can be very simple and become increasingly complex, but means that eventually all components of an instructional process be considered and evaluated in program development, with particular emphasis on the relative cost of particular components. Educators need to move toward a cost effectiveness approach to program development in school systems, and the full disclosure of performance is a very necessary step. It can be said with honesty that the school system runs greater dangers of public misunderstanding by keeping important information from the public than by disclosing it.

Public Relations Applications Based on Integrated CAS Findings

Financial planning and release of financial information related to curriculum and evaluation can be a very difficult process since most people are not aware of all of the components involved. Illus. 9-6 is an example of the way that a school system can explain the fiscal year and factors affecting financial forecasting in graphic form as part of its CAS development program.

Illus. 9-6 goes far toward explaining the complicated system of school financing and its relation to other factors, such as teacher contracts, master contracts with employees, and tax receipts.

Ideally, the Board, central administration, building administration and staff should have a thorough knowledge of curriculum, school finance and evaluation. Such knowledge comes in several ways. For example, an interesting side benefit to negotiations has been the greater awareness and understanding of school finance on the part of the teacher and operating

WHY FISCAL PLANNING FOR THE PUBLIC SCHOOLS IS COMPLICATED

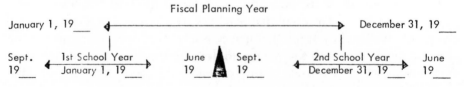

Fiscal Planning Year

FACTORS TO CONSIDER:

1. Funds must be appropriated for the period from January 1, to December 31.

2. Funds must be budgeted for the period from July 1, to June 30.

3. Children attend school from September to June.

4. Every school year involves two different fiscal years.

5. Teachers are contracted for a 186 day school year from September to June.

6. Teachers' salaries must be paid from two different fiscal years.

7. Staff salaries represent 80% of all operating expenses of the school district.

8. It is extremely difficult to adjust programs at mid-year in January when the new fiscal period starts, because of teacher contract obligations assumed in September.

9. Public schools receive funds from local taxes, state taxes and Federal taxes all of which have different collection procedures and are re-distributed to our schools according to different formulas during the four fiscal periods of the year. All of which means that it is complicated to know exactly what funds are available, and when.

Illus. 9-6

employee organizations, and its application to other areas of school operation. CAS has the potential for aiding the negotiation process and contributing further to financial knowledge, particularly if teaching and operating employees are involved in the development of CAS.

Earlier in the chapter, comparing costs with student skills, and the release of such information, was discussed at length. Illus. 9-7 shows how a school system using CAS took the expressed goals of students' future plans and compared these goals with the way funds were being expended. The expenditure figure was derived by compiling a list of the courses which students would normally be taking to achieve one of the goals expressed, such as college or immediate employment, finding the total cost as derived by CAS, and then finding the percentage of the total cost of operating the high school program these programs represent. Illus. 9-7 shows that expenditures were quite close to the expressed students' goals. However, if these expressed goals are correct, it is apparent that continued study should be given to further district adjustments of college and immediate employment course expenditure.

PREVIEW OF FUTURE COST REPORTING TECHNIQUES

The following is a comparison of the Guidance Department's Report on Anytown High School 19___ Graduates and the Cost of Providing the Desired Training Indicated.

Area Studied	Students' Goals	Our Cost	How We Spend
1. College Bound	58%	$631,361.88	61%
2. Technical 8% Business 6% Nursing 2%	16%	196,653.70	19%
3. Immediate Employment	12%	93.151.75	9%
4. Armed Services 4% Marriage 3% Travel & Undecided 7%	14%	113,852.14	11%
	100%	$1,035,019.47 [1]	100%

Illus. 9-7

Illus. 9-8 details further how a school system developed a CAS achievement cost index analysis using standardized tests and applied guidelines for release of such information explained earlier in this chapter. Illus. 9-8 indicates the way that a school organization can take readily available information from their testing program, apply a CAS analysis to test results, and arrive at conclusions which can be communicated to the Board, school employees, administration and the public.

---

[1]This figure represents the total cost of operating the present program at the Anytown High School for one complete school year (including three months summer maintenance).

AN ACHIEVEMENT COST INDEX ANALYSIS

Test Instruments Included

Achievement Test – Grade 6 Level, Based upon 46,000 Sixth Grade Students, Nationwide Reliability Determined to be 88%

Comprehensive Tests of Basic Skills – Grade 6 Level, Based upon 170,000 Sixth Grade Students, Nationwide Reliability Determined to be 93%

The Anytown School District standardized testing program is designed to compare the achievement of Anytown students of the Kindergarten, 4th, 6th, 8th and 10th grade levels with the achievement of students of those levels throughout our nation.

Below are some of our results and the approximate cost to the Anytown Citizens of this achievement.

Results and Cost

Area	National Average Achievement	Anytown Average Achievement	
Reading Achievement	6th	6.6 grade, Our sixth graders are generally six months ahead of the National Average.[2]	$33,160.80
Reading Vocabulary	6th	6.6 grade, Anytown is 6 months ahead of the National Average	16,580.40
Reading Comprehension	6th	6.9 grade, Anytown is 9 months ahead of the National Average	16,580.40
Language Mechanics	6th	6.7 grade, Anytown is 7 months ahead of the National Average	33,160.80
Arithmetic Concepts	6th	6.8 grade, Anytown is 8 months ahead of the National Average	13,264.32
Arithmetic Application	6th	6.9 grade, Anytown is 9 months ahead of the National Average	13,264.32

Illus. 9-8

[2]In 19-- these same students were one month below the third grade National Average.

Illus. 9-9 is the next step in reporting test information by developing a dual comparison. In part one, the CAS analysis is given by school and test scores. Part two of the analysis shows comparisons by school, cost and number of students. Note the variations of cost and achievement in both analyses. Illus. 9-5, "School District Human and Financial Information,"

A COMPARISON OF STUDENT ACHIEVEMENT AND RELATED COSTS

Kindergarten Achievement/Cost Statement Based Upon the Report on Kindergarten Achievement, May _____

Test Instrument Used

Reading Readiness Test – Kindergarten Level Test, Based upon 12,225 Kindergarten Age Students, Nationwide Reliability Determined to be 85% – Copyright Date, 19___

School	National Average Score	Anytown 19___ Average Score	Number of Months Our Students are Ahead of the National Average Reading Readiness
Anson	55	56	One month
Central	55	63	Eight months
Center	55	60	Five months
Dobson	55	62	Seven months
East	55	62	Seven months
Ertil	55	61	Six months
Gateway	55	68	One year
Harvey	55	63	Eight months
West	55	55	at National Level

School	Our Cost	Number of Teachers	Number of Students	Per Pupil Cost
Anson	$ 8,639.42	1/2	34	$ 254.10
Central	6,615.76	1/2	32	206.75
Center	13,166.24	1	42	313.49
Dobson	11,731.59	1	61	192.33
East	12,001.49	1	62	193.58
Ertil	12,273.43	1	52	236.03
Gateway	14,864.43	1	48	309.68
Harvey	7,382.58	1/2	33	223.72
West	12,422.05	1	42	295.76
	$99,096.99 [3]	7 1/2	406	

Illus. 9-9

[3]Teachers with more experience and more educational preparation are paid higher salaries, thus the resulting cost difference.

details the major source of such variations and will add greatly to the explanation of these differences. The footnote in Illus 9-5 highlights the major source of such variation—teacher experience and education level.

There are differences of opinion regarding the manner in which a particular school system should use CAS data. This is as it should be, since once a CAS management information system is developed and applied by using the procedures set forth in this book, then it becomes the responsibility of the individual, the administration, the Board, the school system and the public to interpret and apply the data which is produced. The important part of the whole process is that a systems approach is developed, and that a systematic, planned, regular analysis is instituted. CAS should, at the very least, help point up the problems facing school systems and provide a far better analysis tool than has ever been available to most educators in the past.

Start with the Known

Obviously you do not introduce CAS in a vacuum. You must be thoroughly familiar with the existing local situation. Understanding that system is a primary prerequisite. To violate a community's shared values and objectives is to virtually ensure the failure of CAS.

By relating the CAS to the existing situation, the innovation may be seen as having a central bearing on the actual local situation. Pinpoint the problem situations and involve key publics in the process—then plan action.

First, build links in an action and communication network. Too frequently programs fail because of unwillingness or delay on the part of the initiators to involve others in the work of the program.

Second, get commitments for action. Programs often seem to lose momentum following the definition of need. People agree that problems exist and that something should be done to remedy them, but the required action steps are never taken. To avoid this, get commitments for action from people whose participation is essential to the success of the program.

Third, mobilize your resources. Launch the communication program. Take action steps.

Fourth, extend the action and communication network. Having defined the problem and initiated action to deal with it, take your program and your message to a larger audience. In the process, alleviate fears of change and explain to the larger community the ways in which change through CAS will be beneficial.

Fifth, evaluate what is happening continually and objectively. Don't allow yourself to see only the favorable developments and overlook the unfavorable ones which need attention.

Sixth, be open to an alternate course of action. At any point in any action there exists the possibility that alternate courses of action may prove better than the ones you started with. After all, change is not sought for change's sake. The development of CAS is based on the assumption that we can eliminate or alleviate certain problems which exist in the education system.

Summary

Once the public and the school staff begin to think in terms of a cost accountability system, the results of programs and the instructional process will become more effective. The experience in many school systems using CAS bears out this hypothesis.

In the past, requests have been made for lump sum, across the board reductions in school programs, or across the board lump sum requests for additional programs. It is very difficult to assign any kind of qualitative or cost analysis to requests made in this fashion.

The CAS approach provides information to allow for the identification of specific services which should be added or curtailed, or lost or gained, as a result of a particular budget. There is no question that the public is willing to support increases or reductions when they recognize the value of the specific services involved. Integration of the fiscal plan with the educational program allows Boards and administrators to go to the taxpayers with a budget which they can defend as fiscally responsible, and explain it in terms which can be understood.

As the staffs of school systems sharpen their capabilities in the utilization of CAS, the benefits increase. More specifically, it is anticipated that once long range objectives and priorities have been established under a management system such as CAS, the district will be able to relate its negotiations to the stated, organizational objectives. Teacher and operating employee demands, for example, can be related to the objectives of the school district and will facilitate the achievement of these objectives.

There are many additional uses of CAS, such as in the area of capital outlay, unification of school districts, reorganization of specialized educational services and intergovernmental relationships at the county, state and even national level. As more school systems adopt CAS, uses will be greatly expanded, for it is a viable system of management. Of all the possible applications of CAS, one of the most significant to school systems is its utilization as a vehicle for organizing and explaining data to overcome taxpayer resistance to school budgets and, as a result, increasing the credibility of educators.

APPENDIX A

COST ACCOUNTABILITY CODING SYSTEM

Object	Level I[1] Function	Scope	Level II Program	Level III Building	Level IV Grade	Level V (Opt.) Course
XX	XXX	X	XX	XX	XX	XXX

Example:

A	16a	1	11	61	10	(to de developed)
Salary	Teachers Summer School	Regular	Math	Senior High School	10th Grade	Algebra I

---

[1]Level I is state mandated accounting system. See Auditor of State of Ohio, Form 84, (Rev. 10-61) for complete explanation.

Note: "X" indicates number of digits in code group.

ANYTOWN SCHOOL DISTRICT
PROGRAM COST ACCOUNTABILITY SYSTEM 19--

Level I to Level II

Level I / Level II	Coordination 36,500.00	Instruction 471,087.00	Coordinate Act. 21,200.00	Auxiliary Ser. 46,120.00	Operation. Plant 44,300.00
Art	1,423.50	23,380.50	826.80	1,798.68	1,805.70
Program Records (Atten. Grades etc.)	1,861.50	30,574.50	1,081.20	2,352.12	2,361.30
Business Education	1,058.50	17,385.50	614.80	1,337.48	1,342.70
Drivers Education	146.00	2,398.00	84.80	184.48	185.20
Foreign Language	584.00	9,592.00	339.20	737.92	740.80
Home Economics	1,095.00	17,985.00	636.00	1,383.60	1,389.00
Industrial Arts	657.00	10,791.00	381.60	830.16	833.40
Kindergarten	985.50	16,186.50	572.40	1,245.24	1,250.10
Language Arts	8,687.00	14,268.00	5,045.60	10,976.56	11,019.40
Mathematics	4,015.00	65,945.00	2,332.00	5,073.20	5,093.00
Library	803.00	13,189.00	466.40	1,014.64	1,018.60
Music	1,387.00	22,781.00	805.60	1,752.56	1,759.40
Physical Education	1,861.50	30,574.50	1,081.20	2,352.12	2,361.30
Distributive Education	1,387.00	22,781.00	805.60	1,752.56	1,759.40
Science & Health	3,285.00	53,955.00	1,908.00	4,150.80	4,167.00
Social Studies	2,920.00	47,960.00	1,696.00	3,689.60	3,704.00
Student Activities	547.50	8,992.50	318.00	691.80	694.50
Machine Shop	1,752.00	28,776.00	1,017.60	2,213.76	2,222.40
EMR Programs	2,044.00	33,572.00	1,187.20	2,582.72	2,592.80
TOTAL	36,500.00	471,087.00	21,200.00	46,120.00	44,300.00

Appendix B (Con't.)

Special Ser. 1,800.00	Supplies 74,500.00	Maintenance Mat. 6,000.00	Equip. Rep. 14,800.00	Contract Open Order 51,300.00	Fixed Ugs. 151,500.00	Contingent 7,200.00
70.20	2,905.50	234.00	577.20	2,000.70	5,908.50	280.80
91.80	3,799.50	306.00	754.80	2,616.30	7,726.50	367.20
52.20	2,160.50	174.00	429.20	1,487.70	4,393.50	208.80
7.20	298.00	24.00	59.20	205.20	606.00	28.80
28.80	1,192.00	96.00	236.80	820.80	2,424.00	115.20
54.00	2,235.00	180.00	444.00	1,539.00	4,545.00	216.00
32.40	1,341.00	108.00	266.40	923.40	2,727.00	125.60
48.60	2,011.50	162.00	399.60	1,385.10	4,090.50	194.40
428.40	17,731.00	1,428.00	3,522.40	12,209.40	36,057.00	1,713.60
198.00	8,195.00	660.00	1,628.00	5,643.00	16,665.00	792.00
39.60	1,639.00	132.00	325.60	1,128.60	3,333.00	158.40
68.40	2,831.00	228.00	562.40	1,949.40	5,757.00	273.60
91.80	3,799.50	306.00	754.80	2,616.30	7,726.50	367.20
68.40	2,831.00	228.00	562.40	1,949.40	5,757.00	273.60
162.00	6,705.00	540.00	1,332.00	4,617.00	13,635.00	648.00
144.00	5,960.00	480.00	1,184.00	4,104.00	12,120.00	576.00
27.00	1,117.50	90.00	222.00	769.50	2,272.50	108.00
86.40	3,576.00	288.00	710.40	2,462.40	7,272.00	345.60
100.80	4,172.00	336.00	828.80	2,872.80	8,484.00	403.20
1,800.00	74,500.00	6,000.00	14,800.00	51,300.00	151,500.00	7,200.00

Appendix B (Con't.)

Capital Outlay	Debt Service	Total
23,000.00	70,200.00	1,149,920.00
897.00	2,737.80	44,846.88
1,173.00	3,580.20	58,645.92
667.00	2,035.80	33,347.68
92.00	280.80	4,599.68
368.00	1,123.20	18,398.72
690.00	2,106.00	34,497.60
414.00	1,263.60	20,698.56
621.00	1,895.40	31,047.84
5,474.00	16,707.60	273,680.96
2,530.00	7,722.00	126,491.20
506.00	1,544.40	25,298.24
874.00	2,667.60	43,696.96
1,173.00	3,580.20	58,645.92
874.00	2,667.60	43,696.96
2,070.00	6,318.00	103,492.80
1,840.00	5,616.00	91,993.60
345.00	1,053.00	17,248.80
1,104.00	3,369.60	55,196.16
1,288.00	3,931.20	64,395.52
23,000.00	70,200.00	1,149,920.00

APPENDIX C

ANYTOWN SCHOOL DISTRICT
PROGRAM COST ACCOUNTABILITY SYSTEM

Level II to Level III

Level III \ Level II	Art 44,846.88	Program Records 58,645.92	Bus. Educ. 33,347.68	Drivers Ed. 4,599.68	Foreign Lang. 18,398.72	Home Economics 34,497.60	Ind. Arts 20,698.56
Elementary K-6	23,320.38	30,495.88	17,340.79	2,391.83	9,567.33	17,938.75	10,763.25
Jr. High 7 & 8	7,175.50	9,383.35	5,335.63	735.95	2,943.80	5,519.62	3,311.77
High School 9-12	14,351.00	18,766.69	10,671.26	1,471.90	5,887.59	11,039.23	6,623.54
Total	44,846.88	58,645.92	33,347.68	4,599.68	18,398.72	34,497.60	20,698.56

176

Appendix C (Con't.)

Kindergarten 31,047.84	Language Arts 273,680.96	Math. 126,491.20	Library 25,298.24	Music 43,696.96	Phy. Ed. 58,645.92	Dist. Ed. 43,696.96	Science & Health 103,492.80	Soc. Studies 91,993.60
16,144.88	142,314.10	65,775.42	13,155.08	22,722.42	30,495.88	22,722.42	53,816.25	47,836.67
4,967.65	43,788.95	20,238.59	4,047.72	5,991.51	9,383.35	6,991.51	16,558.85	14,718.98
9,935.31	87,577.91	40,477.19	8,095.44	13,983.03	18,766.69	13,983.03	33,117.70	29,437.95
31,047.84	273,680.96	126,491.20	25,298.24	43,696.96	58,645.92	43,696.96	103,492.80	91,993.60

Student Activities 17,248.80	Machine Shop 55,196.16	EMR Prog. 64,395.52	TOTAL 1,149,920.00
8,969.38	28,702.00	33,485.67	597,958.38
2,759.90	8,831.39	10,303.28	183,987.20
5,519.62	17,662.77	20,606.57	367,974.42
17,248.80	55,196.16	64,395.52	1,149,920.00

ANYTOWN SCHOOL DISTRICT
PROGRAM COST ACCOUNTABILITY SYSTEM

Level III to Level IV

Level III / Level IV	Elementary (K-6) 597,958.38	Jr. High (7-8) 183,987.20	High School (9-12) 367,974.42	Total
Kindergarten	87,301.92			
Grade 1	78,930.51			
Grade 2	84,910.09			
Grade 3	93,281.51			
Grade 4	89,693.76			
Grade 5	80,126.42			
Grade 6	83,714.17			
Grade 7		90,889.68		
Grade 8		93,097.52		
Grade 9			110,392.33	
Grade 10			95,673.35	
Grade 11			74,698.81	
Grade 12			87,209.93	
Total	597,958.38	183,987.20	367,974.42	

ANYTOWN SCHOOL DISTRICT
PROGRAM COST ACCOUNTABILITY SYSTEM

Level IV to Level V

Level V \ Level IV	Kindergarten 87,301.92	Grade 1 78,930.51	Grade 2 84,910.09	Grade 3 93,281.51	Grade 4 89,693.76	Grade 5 80,126.42	Grade 6 83,714.17
Citizenship (Pledge to Flag, etc.)	4,365.10	3,946.52	4,245.50	4,664.08	4,484.69	4,006.32	4,185.71
Reading	31,428.69	28,414.98	28,020.33	27,984.45	24,217.31	15,230.34	20,091.40
Language	2,619.06	2,367.92	2,547.30	3,731.26	5,381.63	5,608.85	5,859.99
Spelling	3,492.08	3,157.22	3,396.40	3,731.26	3,587.75	3,205.06	3,348.57
Handwriting	2,619.06	2,367.92	2,547.30	4,664.07	4,484.69	4,006.32	4,185.71
Math	11,349.25	10,260.97	11,887.41	13,059.41	12,557.13	10,416.44	10,882.84
Soc. Studies	3,492.08	3,157.22	4,245.51	4,456.89	5,381.62	5,608.85	5,859.99
Science Health	4,365.10	3,946.53	5,054.60	4,456.85	8,072.44	8,012.64	8,371.42
Directed Phy. Ed.	4,365.09	3,946.53	4,245.51	4,664.08	4,484.69	4,807.59	5,022.85
Music	4,365.09	3,946.52	4,245.51	4,664.08	4,484.69	4,006.32	4,185.71
Art	4,365.09	3,946.52	4,245.51	4,664.08	2,690.81	2,403.79	2,511.42
Recess	6,984.15	6,314.44	6,792.81	7,462.52	7,175.50	6,410.11	6,697.13
Admin. Work (Grades Attendance)	3,492.08	3,157.22	3,396.40	2,798.44	2,690.81	2,403.79	2,511.43
U. S. History							
Science							
Reading							
English							
Math							
Creative Skills							

Appendix E (Con't.)

Grade 7	Grade 8	Grade 9	Grade 10	Grade 11	Grade 12	TOTAL
90,889.68	93,097.52	110,392.33	95,673.35	74,698.81	87,209.93	
						29,897.92
						179,387.50
						28,116.01
						23,918.34
						24,875.07
						80,413.45
						32,242.16
						42,359.62
						31,536.34
						29,897.92
						24,827.22
						47,836.66
						20,450.17
14,542.35	14,895.60					
14,542.35	14,895.60					
15,451.25	15,826.58					
15,451.25	15,826.58					
15,451.24	15,826.58					
15,451.24	15,826.58					

APPENDIX F

ANYTOWN SCHOOL DISTRICT
PROGRAM COST ACCOUNTABILITY SYSTEM 19--

Level IV to Level V

Enrl.	S	High School Program	Gr.	Grade 9 110,392.33	Grade 10 96,673.35	Grade 11 71,698.81	Grade 12 87,209.93	Total	Per Pupil Cost
15	1	Home Ec. I	9	4,591.32				4,591.32	306.08
19	1	Art I	9	4,591.32				4,591.32	241.64
40	2	Practical Science	9	9,284.67				9,284.67	232.11
34	2	General Science	9	9,284.67				9,284.67	273.07
36	2	Algebra I	9	9,284.67				9,284.67	257.90
51	2	General Math	9	9,284.67				9,284.67	182.05
47	2	9th Girls Health & P.E.	9	9,284.67				9,284.67	197.54
24	1	Spanish I	9	4,693.35				4,693.35	195.55
25	2	Woodworking Ind. Arts	9	9,284.66				9,284.66	371.38
10	1	Latin I	9	4,591.32				4,591.32	459.13
76	3	English 9	9	13,875.98				13,875.98	182.57
50	2	9th Boys Health & P.E.	9	9,284.66				9,284.66	185.69
31	1	General Business	9	4,693.35				4,693.35	151.39
9	1	Home Ec. II	10		4,103.58			4,103.58	455.95
97	4	English 10	10		16,588.96			16,588.96	171.02
20	1	Plane Geometry	10		4,190.90			4,190.90	209.54
38	1	Sr. Band	10		4,190.90			4,190.90	110.28
42	1	10th Girls Phy. Ed.	10		4,190.90			4,190.90	99.78

Appendix F (Con't.)

46	2	Biology	9,294.48	8,294.48	180.31
13	1	Spanish II	4,103.58	4,103.58	315.66
49	2	World History	8,294.48	8,294.48	169.27
24	1	World Geography	4,190.90	4,190.90	174.62
11	1	Latin II	4,103.59	4,103.59	373.05
70	1	10th Boys Phys. Ed.	4,278.20	4,278.20	61.11
31	2	Bookkeeping I	8,294.48	8,294.48	267.56
26	1	Business Math	4,190.90	4,190.90	161.18
52	2	Typing I	8,294.48	8,294.48	159.50
16	7	Machine Shop I	16,694.90	19,694.90	1,230.93
7	1	Home Ec. III	2,813.56	2,813.56	401.93
9	1	Advanced Art	2,813.56	2,813.56	312.61
62	3	English	8,440.67	8,440.67	136.13
25	2	Chemistry	5,627.11	5,627.11	225.08
46	3	Drivers Training	8,440.67	8,440.67	183.49
11	1	Spanish III & IV	2,813.56	2,813.56	255.77
20	1	Metal & Machine Ind. Arts	2,813.56	2,813.56	140.67
67	3	American History	8,440.67	8,440.67	125.98
5	1	Shorthand I	2,813.56	2,813.56	562.71
24	1	Algebra II	2,813.56	2,813.56	117.23
7	1	Typing II	2,813.56	2,813.56	401.93

Appendix F (Con't.)

		Course	Grade					
9	1	Home Ec. IV	12			2,312.17	2,312.17	256.90
6	7	Machine Shop II	12			16,344.69	16,344.69	1,816.07
34	1	English 12	12			2,391.91	2,391.91	70.35
54	2	Sr. English	12			4,624.35	4,624.35	85.63
9	1	Physics	12			2,391.91	2,391.91	265.76
51	1	Sr. High Chorus	12			2,391.91	2,391.91	46.90
21	7	Distributive Education	12			16,344.69	16,344.69	778.31
14	1	Earth Science	12			2,391.91	2,391.91	170.85
17	1	Advanced Biology	12			2,391.91	2,391.91	140.70
19	2	Automotives Ind. Arts	12			4,624.35	4,624.35	243.38
82	3	American Government	12			7,016.25	7,016.25	85.56
15	1	Economics/Sociology	12			2,391.91	2,391.91	155.46
11	1	Speech	12			2,391.91	2,391.91	217.44
20	1	Journalism	12			2,391.91	2,391.91	119.59
7	1	Personal Skills	12			2,312.18	2,312.18	330.31
10	1	Office Practice	12			2,391.91	2,391.91	235.19
9	1	Trig. Adv. Math	12			2,312.18	2,312.18	256.90
2	1	Shorthand II	12			2,312.18	2,312.18	1,156.09
26	2	Special Education	9-12	5,017.81	1,672.60		6,690.41	257.32
33	1	Study Hall (155)	9-12	3,345.21			3,345.21	101.37
24	1	Study Hall (301)	9-12		3,345.21		3,345.21	139.38

Appendix F (Con't.)

70	1	Study Hall (178)	9-12	3,345.21		3,345.21	47.78
61	1	Study Hall (178)	9-12		3,345.21	3,345.21	54.83
57	1	Study Hall (178)	9-12			3,345.21	58.68
41	1	Study Hall (178)	9-12			3,345.21	81.59
1990	110						
		- Chagrin Valley Vocational -					
1	3	Production Agr.	12			93.18	93.18
1	3	O.W.E. Occup. Work Exp.	12			173.28	173.26
1	3	D.C.T. Div. Coop. Train.	12			119.90	119.90
2	3	C.O.E. Coop. Off. Train.	12			199.96	99.98
1	3	Graphics Arts	11		124.99	124.99	124.99
1	3	Child Care	11		139.67	139.67	139.67
1	3	D.C.T.	12		203.00	203.00	203.00
3	3	Cosmetology I	11		750.00	750.00	125.00

TOTAL   367,974.42

APPENDIX G

CAFETERIA COST ANALYSIS

Personnel currently under contract (181 days):

	This Year's Salary	Last Year's Salary
Mrs. Jones	$ 4,968.00	$ 4,700.00
Mrs. Smith	3,752.00	3,550.00
Mrs. Henry	3,858.00	3,650.00
Mrs. Frank (Snack Bar)	4,175.00	3,950.00
Mrs. Williams (Elementary)	3,224.00	1,140.00
TOTAL	$19,977.00	$16,990.00

	— THIS YEAR —			LAST YEAR
	H.S. Cafe	H.S. Snack Bar	Elem. Cafe	H.S. Cafe
Per Day Labor Cost - Contracts (181 Days)	$69.00	$23.00	$17.00	$ 93.00
Student Help[1]	5.00	3.00	3.00	15.00
Total Per Day Labor Cost	$74.00	$26.00	$20.00	$108.00

	This Year	Last Year
Number of meals served from September to May	50,540	28,175

Income Expense Breakdown

	This Year	Last Year
Labor Expense (Actual 181 Days)	21,720.00	19,548.00
Food Expense (Approximately)	11,430.00	15,762.00
Total Meals Served (Actual) to Date	50,540	28,175
Reimbursement at $.08 per meal	4,043.20	2,254.00
Reimbursement at $.50 per free lunch	720.00	450.00
Profit on Meals and Snack Bar	4,885.49	-0-
Total Profit on Program (Approximately)	9,648.69	(10,868.00) Loss

---

[1]These students are not paid this money directly. They earn $.50 per student per day worked, and this money is transferred from the general activity fund account (Board funds) to the activity fund of the account which each student represents. In this way they are earning money for their club or organization by helping the school. Also, they are volunteers doing community service, so the minimum wage does not apply. The state law does restrict these students to one hour maximum work per day on a volunteer basis, therefore, we must keep rotating them from one lunch period to another. The principal keeps an accounting on the time worked by each group. The student council has provided most of the needed labor this year. All groups have been invited to participate.

Appendix G *(Con't.)*

We have not yet completed our year-end inventory, however, I would estimate it to be in the area of $3,000 in food and paper supplies. I hope to reduce the food on hand to around $1,000 during the summer, or about one month of supplies to start next year.

For future information, we have made many menu changes this year. The most successful menus have been:

1.	Pizza	6.	Hamburgers
2.	Spaghetti	7.	Toasted Cheese
3.	Weiners	8.	Fish
4.	Sloppy Joe's	9.	Macaroni & Cheese
5.	Sliced Turkey	10.	Roast Chicken

Of these, hamburgers are the most expensive and only sell if a good grade of hamburger is used. I would suggest that to continue a profitable operation in the future that we concentrate on pizza, spaghetti, weiners (good grade), sliced turkey and roast chicken (only when government provides), sloppy Joe's (with government pork only), and fish and macaroni and cheese occasionally. By limiting our menu to these items, it is possible to keep our inventory low and better control our buying.

To prepare for future growth in our program, however, I would suggest that during the summer we have a new confectionery oven installed to replace one of our old ones at a cost of approximately $2600. We also need one additional chest-type freezer at approximately $380. The addition of these items should carry us for another three to four years' growth.

If we are able to maintain our profit margin next year, we might want to consider lowering the price of lunch once again. However, I think we should see what the summer months do to prices.

I hope you will help me keep this information confidential for several reasons:

1. This is a difficult program to manage, and the more confidential the facts in this report remain, the more difficult it is for someone to influence it.

2. I believe at this point we are recovering from a loss in our program, and to move from such a large loss to a profit in such a short period of time might not look good.

3. If anyone in the community is interested in details concerning our cafeteria program, I would be happy to explain the entire operation.

APPENDIX H

REPORT ON COST OF PRESENT BUILDING MAINTENANCE PROGRAM

RATES

Custodians Under Contract	Av. Hours Each Week	This Year Per Hour	This Year 1½ Time	Last Year Per Hour	Last Year 1½ Time
Mrs. Jones	25	2.43		2.30	
Mrs. Smith	30	2.27			
Mr. James	45	3.12	4.68	2.95	4.43
Mr. Henry	50	3.01	4.51	2.85	4.35
Mr. Williams	53	3.83	5.74	3.62	5.43

Building	High School	Elementary School
Aver. Hrs. Per Week	226	76
Aver. Total Cost Per Week	$577.40	$271.83
Aver. Per Hour Cost	$ 2.55	$ 3.58
Approx. No. People Served	900	300
Approx. Per Student Cost For Maintenance Per Week	$ .64	$ .90
With Williams on High School Maintenance	$ .77	$ .77

Substitute custodians, mostly students, have worked at least some hours as needed at the federal minimum wage per hour, and all of their time is included above. All of these boys have been employed at least a few hours. I believe this program has greatly helped the boys in the community find part-time jobs and also take more pride in their school.

Last year, in addition to Mr. Jones, Mr. & Mrs. James and Mr. Smith, we also had employed on a contractual basis Mr. & Mrs. Henry and Mr. Williams. All of these people were maintaining the high school building only. Their pay rates were as follows:

	Last Year Regular	Last Year 1½ Time
Mrs. Smith	2.30	3.45
Mrs. Jones	2.30	3.45
Mr. Frank	2.62	5.43
Mr. Smith	2.75	4.13
Mr. Jones	2.85	4.35
Mr. Henry	2.95	4.43
Mr. Williams	2.50	3.75

Appendix H *(Con't.)*

Building	High School
Aver. Hrs. Per Week (Regular 238 - 1½ Time 59)	297
Aver. Total Cost Per Week	$868.26
Aver. Per Hour Cost	$ 2.92
Approx. No. People Served	1100
Approx. Per Student Cost For Maintenance Per Week	$ 1.15

Conclusions:

1. Our present program has reduced the cost of maintaining our buildings from $1.15 per week per student to $.77 per week per student. This represents a savings of $.38 per student per week in maintenance, or $.38 x 1100 students x 52 weeks. $21,736.00 approximate yearly salary savings per year.

2. This savings is accomplished in spite of a salary increase of 6%.

3. Along with the savings, we have provided much needed part-time jobs for young boys in the community.

4. Notice also that even though we now have two buildings that our average hours worked to maintain two buildings has only increased from 297 average hours per week to 302 average hours per week. Although the average increase is only five hours that we have more people on the job, the savings results from the lower wages paid to the non-contract substitute custodians.

5. These boys are working under working permits as school employees (not a work-study program) and are covered by workmen's compensation.

6. In my opinion, the building looks better.

7. By centralizing the ordering and control of maintenance supplies, it is my estimation that we have also realized a 20% to 30% reduction in loss of supplies inventory.

Proposal:

On the basis of the above study, I would recommend that we seriously consider the elimination of double contracts for the coming school year.

APPENDIX I

BUILDING FUND REPORT

Balance in Building Fund 3/1/73		$159,013.32
March Warrants		46,514.50
April Warrants		24,008.41
	Balance	88,490.41
Contractors' bills on hand		11,731.50
10% retainer due		42,269.61
Holding invoice		6,400.00
	Balance	28,089.30
Interest received in March		1,983.77
	Balance 5-1-7-	30,073.07

APPROXIMATE BREAKDOWN OF BUILDING FUND EXPENDITURES

Bonds			$615,000.00
Approx. interest earned			15,000.00
			630,000.00
Contractors Final Figures			
Nolan	$ 91,386.00		
Miller Plbg. Htg.	93,595.00		
Smith	287,030.00		
Jones	47,951.00		
Frank	2,559.00		
Smith	33,496.00		
	556,017.00	556,017.00	
		73,983.00	
Old Bldg. Repairs			
Lumber	2,362.85		
Jones	2,619.15		
Window Proj.	19,529.00		
Architect	1,434.00		
Smith	685.00		
	26,630.00	26,630.00	
		47,353.00	
Equipment for new building		16,000.00	
		31,353.00	
Commitment on new window project		9,623.00	
	Balance	21,730.00	

Appendix I *(Con't.)*

EQUIPMENT FOR NEW ELEMENTARY SCHOOL FROM BLDG. FUND

Fair Equipment Company (Desks)	$1,627.40
Beckley-Cardy (Eraser cleaner)	86.50
Smith Hardware (Tools & maintenance items)	398.52
Owens Flooring (Floor tile)	135.00
George Jones (Furniture)	3,993.08
Pollution Packer	1,741.66
Olympic Sport Goods (Equip. for gym)	573.80
Lehman Awning (Equip. for gym)	632.00
Olympic Sport Goods (Equip. for gym)	17.95
Olson Electronics (Intercom)	69.25
Larson Laboratories (Gym)	40.65
Admiral Craft Equipment Co.	132.21
Fair Equipment (Office Desks)	399.00
E. F. Hausermann (Wardrobe units & installation)	6,425.00

$16,272.02

CHANGE ORDERS

Miller Plumbing (For Office area)	$2,000.00
Lake Electric ($687.15 - Light fixtures) ($3,170.00 - Electrical work, office area)	3,857.15
George Smith	290.25
George Brown (Concrete walk)	1,073.00

$7,220.40

APPENDIX J

SUBJECT MATTER AREA COST ANALYSIS
DISTRIBUTIVE EDUCATION

Present Enrollment		Enrollment for Next Year (To Date)	
7	North	4	North
5	South	1	South
5	East	1	East
4	West	1	West
		2	Peach
21	Total	9	Washington
		18	Total

What we get from the State:

State vocational units range from $11,377. to $15,570. per year depending upon teacher certification, size of class and subject area to which the unit is applied. (For example; we get more for a machine shop unit than a D.E. unit.)

Mr. Don Smith, Regional Vocational Education Coordinator set our present D.E. unit at $12,350. However, he indicated that we would receive $6,000 of that figure as part of our regular foundation money regardless of the vocational unit. From this we can conclude the following:

D.E. Receipts:

	From State unit	$6,350.00
16 students x $148.16 =	Tuition from other districts	2,370.56
Total reimbursements for program		$8,720.56

D.E. Expenses:

Salary	13,195.40
Insurance & Retirement $360 + 12.9% = 1702.67........	2,062.67
Mileage..	702.00
Guidance supervision and adm. (including % paid to....	6,120.00 [1]
vocational program)	
Materials, supplies, equipment......................	9,220.00 [1]
Overhead (heat, light, power, trans., building)	12,392.89 [1]
	$43,696.96

Approximate per pupil cost this year - $2,080.80

Approximate per pupil cost next year - $2,508.47

Our cost next year:

To continue housing the program at East School - $45,152.52 (approx.)

To send our students to West School   - $ 450.00

---

[1]These figures are based upon our total program cost analysis and should not be interpreted as actual cost.

APPENDIX K

SECRETARIAL COST ANALYSIS

PAST COST

Smith	$ 4,797	42 weeks x 40 hours = 1680 hours
Jones	8,150	49 weeks x 40 hours = 1960 hours
Williams	7,625	49 weeks x 40 hours = 1960 hours
TOTAL	$20,572	5600 = $3.67

If you add the 4% and 5% raises received, plus the step increase received since these people worked here, the per hour rate would be $23,065 + 5600 = $4.12 current per hour cost for past secretarial and clerk service.

PRESENT COST

Smith	$ 5,260	42 weeks x 40 hours = 1680 hours
Jones	6,913	49 weeks x 40 hours = 1960 hours
Williams	6,287	49 weeks x 40 hours = 1960 hours
Kelly	4,649	42 weeks x 40 hours = 1680 hours
Jones	1,516	42 weeks x 30 hours = 1260 hours
Brown	2,643	42 weeks x 24 hours = 1008 hours
TOTAL	$27,268	9548 = $2.86

Present per hour secretarial cost is $2.86 compared to present per hour cost of past secretarial service of $4.12.

Presently, we are employing 3948 total additional hours of service and at present cost this is an additional expense to us of $7,896 (3948 x $2) present per hour cost of additional service. This is a real bargain.

APPENDIX L

PRIORITY LIST

Item	Approximate Cost
1. Baseball backstop	$ 1,500.00
2. Fence project	500.00
3. Stadium rest rooms	1,000.00
4. New locker rooms by converting existing stage	3,500.00
5. Replace clocks on third floor	800.00
6. Carpeting in three-story structure	4,000.00
7. New window shades - approximately 10 additional rooms	500.00
8. Install lights on outside basketball courts	150.00
9. Relocate playground north of building	1,200.00
10. New classroom furniture - approximately five additional rooms	5,000.00
11. Blacktop area around new building	21,000.00
12. Develop road behind bus garage for additional parking for football	5,000.00
13. Develop road to new baseball area	2,000.00
14. Replace doors on gym	500.00
15. Replace light switches in hallways	50.00
16. Install new light fixtures on second and third floors	4,000.00
17. Paint all rooms on second and third floors	1,000.00
18. Install sneeze guards on cafeteria lines	500.00
19. Install additional exhaust fans	200.00
20. Gym Floor and bleachers	2,500.00
21. Develop a Wrestling Gym	10,000.00
	$64,900.00

APPENDIX M

THE FOLLOWING IS A LIST OF INSTRUCTIONAL PROGRAM
AND SYSTEM-WIDE GROWTH PRIORITIES
FOR THE SCHOOL YEAR

Please order these items according to your opinion of their individual importance.

SYSTEMWIDE PRIORITIES

Rank	No.	Items
	1.	Continued Development of Program Cost Accounting (PPBS)
	2.	Development of a more effective Public Relations Program
	3.	Reorganization of Central Office Personnel and Procedures
	4.	Development of an administrative calendar of events
	5.	Clarification of Curriculum Committee responsibilities
	6.	Clarification of Area Chairman responsibilities
	7.	Determine Objectives for TV development
	8.	Determine Objectives for Economic Education development
	9.	Clarification of our Present Internal Organization Structure
	10.	Development of Levy Strategies and Time Tables
	11.	Organization for more effective Radio Station and Newspaper Utilization
	12.	Clarification of Union authority and communication channels
	13.	Clarification of Administrative Council responsibilities
	14.	Reorganization of "Old Records"
	15.	Plan for the future growth of the "Hot Food" program
	16.	Revision and Development of Recruiting Schedules
	17.	Revision of the Substitute Teacher Accounting procedures
	18.	Completion of our present textbook Inventory Analysis
	19.	Development of our "Community Survey"
	20.	Establishment of North Central finding priorities
	21.	Development of Behavioral Objectives for present programs
	22.	Reorganization of Staff Evaluation System
	23.	Plan for In-Service Training of (staff development)
	24.	Reorganization of Present Bidding Procedures
	25.	Improvement of "Roof Top Unit" Service
	26.	Evaluation of our Transportation System effectiveness
	27.	Re-evaluation of our Present Dress Code
	28.	Re-evaluation of our Present Censorship Procedures

Appendix M *(Con't.)*

INSTRUCTIONAL PROGRAMS

<u>Rank</u>	<u>No.</u>	<u>Subject</u>
	1.	Language Arts
	2.	Mathematics
	3.	Science and Health
	4.	Social Studies
	5.	Child Study Center
	6.	Physical Education
	7.	Art
	8.	Music
	9.	Business Education
	10.	Kindergarten
	11.	Industrial Arts
	12.	Home Economics
	13.	Foreign Language
	14.	Student Activities
	15.	Learning Resource Centers
	16.	Drivers Education
	17.	Vocational Agriculture

APPENDIX N

POSITION: PROJECT DIRECTOR

RESPONSIBILITY; The Project Director is directly responsible for the total activities of the CAS program.

FUNCTION: To coordinate and direct all of the personnel and activities of the CAS program.

TASKS:

1. He will serve as Chairman of the Executive Committee.

2. He will prepare the agenda for the Executive Committee.

3. He will establish the place, date, and time for all meetings of the Executive Committee.

4. He will be responsible for notifying members of the Executive Committee of the time, date, and place of meetings.

5. He will be responsible for inviting guests to the Executive Committee meetings.

6. He will be responsible for the development of all State proposals.

7. He will be responsible for the dispensing of all funds.

8. He will be responsible for corresponding with all individuals outside the school system in connection with the CAS project.

9. He will be responsible for hiring all persons involved in the PPBS project.

10. He will be responsible for maintaining the record of dates and time involved in CAS work.

Appendix N *(Con't.)*

POSITION: SYSTEMS COORDINATOR

RESPONSIBILITY: The Systems Coordinator is directly responsible
                  to the District Coordinator

FUNCTION: To coordinate and generate a systems approach which
                      will assist with the achievement of Program objectives.

TASKS:

1. He will design a Program Coding Structure for Instructional and Non-Instructional Programs and Sub-Programs.

2. He will design the forms for the Program-centered Budget.

3. He will write the procedures for the Program-centered Budget.

4. He will write and list the responsibilities for each individual participating in the formulation of the Program-centered Budget.

5. He will direct and coordinate the development of a Computer Program capable of producing a Budget consistent with the State Numerical Accounting System and/or the Program-centered Budget System.

6. He will design an assessment instrument which will be used to assess the Community in terms of Educational Goals and Educational Organizational Goals.

7. He will assist with the development of Direct Goals.

8. He will direct the activities of the Information Disseminator.

9. He will develop PERT Charts as needed to assist the Executive Committee and/or other personnel connected with the CAS Program.

10. He will supervise Cross Walk Activities.

11. He will make all changes necessary to prepare for the development of a total Budget along Program-centered lines.

12. He will implement and design a Sample Test Program for all Program-centered Budget forms and procedures.

13. He will perform all other tasks as assigned by the Project Director.

Appendix N *(Con't.)*

POSITION: INFORMATION DISSEMINATOR

RESPONSIBILITY: The Information Disseminator is directly responsible
                   to the Systems Coordinator

FUNCTION: To develop and disseminate information concerning the
                   CAS program.

TASKS:

1. He will design information dissemination programs.

2. He will design orientation programs.

3. He will serve as research person for the Executive Committee
   or other personnel involved in the CAS program.

4. He will conduct a vocational survey.

5. He will serve as a member of the citizen's advisory group.

6. He will perform all other tasks as assigned by the Project
   Director.

POSITION: DATA COORDINATOR

RESPONSIBILITY: The Data Coordinator is directly responsible
                   to the District Coordinator

FUNCTION: To coordinate and develop data collection
                   procedures and instruments; and coordinate
                   the actual data and tabulate the results for
                   evaluation.

TASKS:

1. He will design the assessment procedure for the development
   of educational goals and educational organizational goals.

2. He will design the assessment procedures for assessing
   the present program structure.

3. He will design the data collection system.

4. He will design a survey system.

5. He will conduct surveys as needed.

6. He will tabulate collected data.

7. He will recommend indicators to the Executive Committee.

8. He will perform all other tasks as assigned by the Project
   Director.

Appendix N *(Con't.)*

POSITION: PROGRAM ANALYST

RESPONSIBILITY: The Program Analyst is directly responsible to
                   the District Coordinator

FUNCTION: To coordinate the development of goals and
                   objectives for the programs and special programs
                   in the system.

TASKS:

1. He will write the district goals for the school system.

2. He will write the educational organizational goals for the
   school system.

3. He will write the goals and objectives for noninstructional
   programs.

4. He will evaluate data collected in terms of their effect
   on goals.

5. He will write the goals and terminal objectives for the
   Kindergarten - 12 Mathematics program.

6. He will assess the present instructional and noninstructional
   Programs.

7. He will evaluate the present programs.

8. He will perform all other tasks as assigned by the Project
   Director.

POSITION: ELEMENTARY ANALYST

RESPONSIBILITY: The Elementary Analyst is directly responsible
                   to the Program Analyst

FUNCTION: To assist with the coordination of the development
                   of goals and objectives for the programs and special
                   programs in the system.

TASKS:

1. He will assist with the writing of the district goals for the
   school system.

2. He will assist with the writing of the educational organizational
   goals for the school system.

3. He will assist with the writing of the goals and objectives for
   non-instructional programs.

4. He will assist with the evaluation of data collected in terms
   of their effect on goals.

Appendix N *(Con't.)*

5. He will assist with the writing of the goals and terminal objectives for the Kindergarten - 12 Mathematics program.

6. He will assist with the assessment of the present instructional and non-instructional programs.

7. He will assist with the evaluation of the present programs.

8. He will perform all other tasks as assigned by the Project Director.

POSITION: SECONDARY ANALYST

RESPONSIBILITY: The Secondary Analyst is directly responsible to the Program Analyst.

FUNCTION: To assist with the coordination of the development of goals and objectives for the programs and special programs in the system.

TASKS:

1. He will assist with the writing of the district goals for the school system.

2. He will assist with the writing of the educational organizational goals for the school system.

3. He will assist with the writing of the goals and objectives for non-instructional programs.

4. He will assist with the evaluation of data collected in terms of their effect on goals.

5. He will assist with the writing of the goals and terminal objectives for the Kindergarten - 12 Mathematics program.

6. He will assist with the assessment of the present instructional and non-instructional programs.

7. He will assist with the evaluation of the present programs.

8. He will perform all other tasks as assigned by the Project Director.

APPENDIX O

ORGANIZATION OF INSTRUCTIONAL TEAM
FOR A MEDIUM SIZE CITY[1]

PURPOSE: To define the responsibilities, structures and methods of operation
             of the Curriculum Council as an integral part of the instructional
             team.

PARTICIPANTS: Superintendent of Schools
                  Deputy Superintendent
                  Assistant Superintendent for Instruction
                  Instructional Administration
                  Certified Staff

FORMS: Submission Form for Curriculum or Instructional Study Proposals
           Initial Report
           Interim Report
           Final Report
           Proposed Course and/or Program Format

Authority of the Council: Recognizing that the educational goals and objectives of the
community and school district may become actualities only through the successful
functioning of the individual classrooms, the Board of Education delegates through the
Superintendent to the Assistant Superintendent for Instruction and Curriculum Council
the responsibility for an on-going appraisal and up-grading of the instructional and
curricular programs and practices. Included in this responsibility is that of providing
additional training or re-training of the professional staff through appropriate in-service
experiences when necessary.

Membership:

Chairman: Assistant Superintendent for Instruction (or his designee)
              12 Administrators (including chairman)
              12 Certified Teachers

---

[1]The author is indebted to the Plymouth Community School District for this format.

Appendix O *(Con't.)*

Functions:

1.   Develop the format to be used in the submission of suggested curriculum and
       instructional studies including objectives and evaluative procedures.

2.   Collect potential problems for curriculum studies from administrators, other professional
       staff members, students, citizens, etc.

3.   Review all suggested studies, establish annual study priorities and respond in writing
       to all properly submitted requests.

4.   Organize Study-Action Committees for the pursuance of designated studies each year.

5.   Establish study procedures and deadlines.

6.   Provide for meeting time for curriculum-instructional studies and for in-service training
       activities.

7.   Formulate budget requests and fund allocations for curriculum development.

8.   Plan for summer curriculum studies.

9.   Receive, evaluate and transmit the findings and curriculum recommendations of the
       Study-Action Committees to the Superintendent of Schools and Board of Education.

10.   Evaluate existing curriculum. Report recommendations for revision in writing to the
       Board of Education through the Assistant Superintendent for Instruction.

11.   Review and evaluate all textbook selection and revisions and recommend to the
       Assistant Superintendent for Instruction approval for Board adoption.

Study-Action Committees:

Membership: Committee members to be appointed annually by the Curriculum Council.

Selections to be made prior to June (except in unusual circumstances) with tenure to
commence with summer curriculum studies and/or the following school year. The committee
chairmen, selected by the C.C., will in turn select committee members in consultation with the
Chairman of the C.C. The C.C. may provide a list of suggested members to the Study
Committee Chairmen. All committee appointments are for the life of the particular study.
The number of members on any given Study-Action Committee will be that deemed appropriate
by the C.C. and will be representative of the school level or levels concerned.

Functions:

1.   Conduct continuing evaluations of the program represented, K-12.

2.   Review textbooks and other instructional materials. Recommend studies leading
       to new adoptions and acquisitions.

3.   Recommend program changes to the Curriculum Council (course additions and
       deletions and changes in program content and methods.)

4.   Prepare course syllabi and teaching guides for use of teaching staff.

Appendix O *(Con't.)*

5.   Plan in-service training activities for total staff of program represented.

6.   Recommend summer curriculum workshops -- define purposes, designate meeting
      dates and locations and select participants.

Each committee shall formulate specific program objectives. These objectives are to be
written in terms of learning outcomes which are measurable. It is expected that each
committee will develop a specific plan for long-range program improvement.

Role of Administrators in Curriculum Development: The Assistant Superintendent for
Instruction will perform coordinating functions in the district-wide studies. He will
chair the Curriculum Council (or his designee). The Assistant Superintendent for Instruction
may initiate requests for program improvement funds for special activities related to curriculum
improvement.

The building principals will provide direct leadership to the grade level and department
groups, will serve as members of the Curriculum Council representing their school level
and will have representation on the Curriculum Council. Principals are ex-offcio members
of all Study-Action Committees. Principals will provide leadership to their building staffs
in the improvement of building programs and may initiate requests for program improvement
funds to conduct building-level studies, pilot programs and in-service training activities.

Directors will serve as chairmen or members of Study Committees representing their respective
programs. Directors may initiate requests for program improvements funds for studies, pilot
programs and in-service training activities for their own departmental staffs.

The Assistant Superintendent for Instruction will receive all recommendations for program
changes from the Curriculum Council. Prior to his personal action on the recommendations
and their transmittal to the Board of Education he will consult the Administrative Advisory
Council when members are available for their reaction to each of the recommendations.

Program Improvement Funds: Requests for program improvement funds are acceptable from the
following sources only: Study Committee Chairmen, Principals, Directors, Assistant
Superintendent for Instruction and the Superintendent of Schools. The C.C. Chairman may
approve requests, within the approved budget, which do not exceed $100 and require
immediate action. Other requests shall be referred to the C.C. for approval.

In-Service and Curriculum Development Time Allotment: An allocation of paid in-service
hours may be made available at the discretion of the Curriculum Council, within the
approved budget. Such hours to include paid substitute time, university or other courses
conducted by experts, carefully approved conferences and conventions for selected
representatives from various disciplines within the district, etc.

It should not be inferred from the allocation of such paid in-service hours that they will
necessarily be used up in a given year. Total hours used will be at the discretion of the
Curriculum Council based on the identified needs of the district and the progress reports
of the various Study-Action Committees throughout the year.

In the event that additional paid in-service hours over and above those budgeted for
a given year appear necessary in the course of an extensive study, request for such hours
shall be made by the Curriculum Council through the Superintendent to the Board of Education.
Judgment to be based on availability of funds.

Appendix O *(Con't.)*

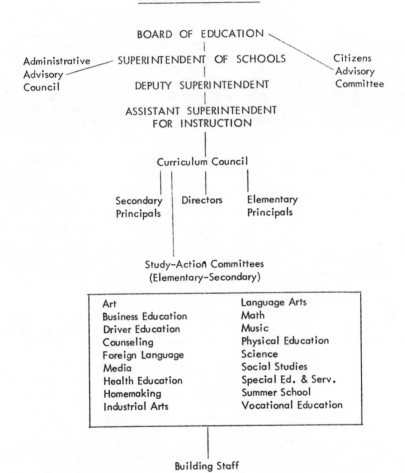

ORGANIZATION CHART

BOARD OF EDUCATION

Administrative   SUPERINTENDENT OF SCHOOLS   Citizens
Advisory   Advisory
Council   DEPUTY SUPERINTENDENT   Committee

ASSISTANT SUPERINTENDENT
FOR INSTRUCTION

Curriculum Council

Secondary   Directors   Elementary
Principals   Principals

Study–Action Committees
(Elementary–Secondary)

Art	Language Arts
Business Education	Math
Driver Education	Music
Counseling	Physical Education
Foreign Language	Science
Media	Social Studies
Health Education	Special Ed. & Serv.
Homemaking	Summer School
Industrial Arts	Vocational Education

Building Staff

Appendix O *(Con't.)*

CURRICULUM COUNCIL

SUBMISSION FORM FOR CURRICULUM OR INSTRUCTIONAL STUDY PROPOSALS

The following guidelines are set up for the purpose of aiding the Curriculum Council to prioritize suggested curriculum and instructional studies.

Please complete the outline below for your proposed curriculum or instructional study, including as much of the following information as possible and including any other data which may be pertinent to the proposal. Please submit 36 duplicated copies of this outline to your building C.C. Representative or the Assistant Superintendent for Instruction.

I.   Name of the person(s) submitting this proposal:

II.   The proposal:

III.   Objectives of the proposed study:

IV.   Number of persons to be involved in the study (estimated):

V.   Schools and/or departments to be represented in the proposed study:

VI.   Financial estimate for the proposed study:

      1.   Release time (number of persons and number of hours):

      2.   Consultants requested and their approximate fees:

      3.   Clerical services and printing:

      4.   Others:

VII.   Additional comments on the proposed study (please use reverse side):

Appendix O *(Con't.)*

CURRICULUM COUNCIL

INITIAL REPORT

Due November 30, 197 ___ , by liaison person to Study-Action Committee and
Curriculum Council.

Name of the Study-Action Committee: _____

Roster of all members:

NAME	SCHOOL
1.	
2.	
3.	
4.	
5.	
6.	
7.	
8.	
9.	
10.	
11.	
12.	
13.	
14.	
15.	
16.	
17.	
18.	

Budget Allocation: _____ (to be filled in by Liaison person)

Approximate budget division as determined by the Study-Action Committee:
      Substitutes   _____
      Consultants   _____
      Clerical   _____
      Travel Expenses   _____
      Other   _____

Proposed meeting dates as determined by the Study-Action Committee:
_____   PLEASE DO NOT SEND SUBSTITUTES FOR
_____   STUDY-ACTION COMMITTEE MEMBERS TO
_____   MEETINGS.

Appendix O *(Con't.)*

CURRICULUM COUNCIL INTERIM REPORT

Due January 15, 197___

Name of Study-Action Committee: _____

Number of study sessions: _____

Number of visitations: _____

Number of consultants: _____

Names of consultants: _____

_____

Amount of budgeted monies used to date:

    Substitutes ($26 per day) and/or $5.25
      reimbursed time to Study-Action
      Committee Members   _____

    Travel Expenses   _____

    Consultant Fees   _____

    Clerical   _____

    Other (please identify)   _____

    Progress Report: This can be in narrative form and include such items as
                     would clarify the steps which this Study-Action Committee
                     has taken toward its goal.

Appendix O *(Con't.)*

<u>CURRICULUM COUNCIL</u>

<u>FINAL REPORT</u>

Due January 15, 197___ if monies are to be requested for implementation during the 19___ - ___ school year.

Otherwise due May 1, 197___ .

Name of Study-Action Committee: _____

Number of study sessions: _____

Number of visitations: _____

Number of consultants: _____

Names of consultants: _____

_____

_____

Amount of budgeted monies used to date:
    Substitutes   _____
    Travel Expenses   _____
    Consultant Fees   _____
    Clerical   _____
    Others (identify)   _____

    TOTAL   _____

Final Report: This should be submitted on the Proposed Course and/or Program Format

Appendix O *(Con't.)*

CURRICULUM COUNCIL

PROPOSED COURSE AND/OR PROGRAM FORMAT

I.   Title of course and/or program

II.   Subject area and grade level of course and/or program

III.   Description of course and/or program (new or revised from the original as needed)

IV.   Course and/or program objectives (stated in measurable, behavioral terms)

V.   Suggested semester outline (when applicable)

VI.   Evaluation procedures for course and/or program (correlated with the objectives)

VII.   Bibliography of recommended professional readings on proposed course and/or program

VIII.   Implementation recommendations:

    A.   Instructional materials needed to implement course and/or program

        1.   Printed materials

            a. Basic and co-basic textbooks
            b. Supplementary reading materials (books, newspapers, periodicals, reprints, articles, etc.)

        2.   Audio-visual materials

            a. Films
            b. Filmstrips
            c. Slides
            d. Recordings
            e. Tapes
            f. Video Tapes
            g. Other

        3.   Other educational aids and equipment

    B.   Additional certified and/or classified staff needed to implement course and/or program

    C.   Staff in-service education needed to implement course and/or program

        1.   Number of staff to be involved (specify teachers, administrators, educational aides, others)

        2.   Number and type of training sessions needed (describe)

        3.   Consultant service required (specify names of consultants if pertinent)

    D.   Special facilities needed to implement course and/or program

    E.   Estimated budget needed to fund each of A-D above.

IX.   Other pertinent information

TEACHER UNIT DISTRIBUTION BY PROGRAM AND SCHOOL

PROGRAM	ELEMENTARY		TU[1]	MIDDLE SCHOOLS				TU[1]
				East	West	North	South	
Art	6.5	3% of 167.5 = 5.025	11.525	2	2	2	2	8
Bus. Ed.								
Comm. Serv.[2]		44% of 11440 = .45	.45		24% of 6240 = .25			.25
Driver Ed.								
For. Lang.								
Home Ec.				1.5	2	2	1.5	7
Ind. Ed.				1	2	2	2	7
Kdg.	18.5		18.5					
Lang. Arts		50% of 167.5 = 83.75	83.75					
English				3.5	2	5.5	2	13
6th Grade				0	30% of 6	0	30% of 6	3.6
Read. Improve.	10		10	1	1	1	1	4
Math		20% of 167.5 = 33.5	33.5	4	3.5	4.5	2.5	14.5
6th Grade				0	30% of 6	0	30% of 6	3.6
Multi-Media	9.5		9.5	1	1	1	1	4
Music	6.5	1% of 167.5 = 1.675	8.175	2	3	2.5	2.5	10
Phys. Ed.	6.5	2% of 167.5 = 3.35	9.85	2	2	2	2	8
Pupil Pers.								
Counselor	1		1	1	1	1	1	4
Spec. Ed.	5		5		2			2
Specialists		60% of 11 = 6.6	6.6		25% of 11 = 2.75			2.75
School Farm		44% of .65 = .286	.286		24% of .65 = .156			.156
Science		10% of 167.5 = 16.75	16.75	3.5	2	3.5	2	11
6th Grade				0	20% of 6	0	20% of 6	2.4
Social Studies		15% of 167.5 = 25.125	25.125	4	2	5.5	2	13.5
6th Grade				0	20% of 6	0	20% of 6	2.4
Voc. Ed.								
TOTALS			240.011					121.156

[1]Teacher Units
[2]See p. 216 for calculation method.

Appendix P *(Con't.)*

TEACHER UNIT DISTRIBUTION BY PROGRAM AND SCHOOL

PROGRAM	HIGH SCHOOLS Washington	Lincoln	TU [1]	TU [2] TOTAL	ROUNDED % APPLIED LEVEL I	to LEVEL II
Art	2	5	7	26.525	5.0	
Bus. Ed. [2]	6	7.5	13.5	13.5	2.6	
Comm. Serv. [2]	32% of $8320 = .33		.33	1.03	.2	
Driver Ed.	$21,000		.85	.85	.2	
For. Lang.	4.5	4	8.5	8.5	1.6	
Home Ec.	2	3	5	12	2.3	
Ind. Ed.	2	7	9	16	3.0	
Kdg.				18.5	3.5	
Lang. Arts				83.75	15.8 ⎱	
English	11.5	14.5	26	39	7.4 ⎬ 23.9	
6th Grade				3.6	.7 ⎰	
Read. Improve.	1	2	3	17	3.2	
Math	9.5	9	18.5	66.5	12.6 ⎱	
6th Grade				3.6	.7 ⎬ 13.3	
Multi-Media	2	2	4	17.5	3.3	
Music	1	3	4	22.175	4.2	
Phys. Ed.	–	10	10	27.85	5.3	
Pupil Pers.						
Counselor	3	6	9	14	2.6 ⎱	
Spec. Ed.	2	–	2	9	1.7 ⎬ 6.4	
Specialists	15% of 11 = 1.65		1.65	11	2.1 ⎰	
School Farm	32% of .65 = .208		.208	.65	.1	
Science	6	7.5	13.5	41.25	7.8 ⎱ 8.3	
6th Grade				2.4	.5 ⎰	
Social Studies	6	11	17	55.625	10.5 ⎱ 11.0	
6th Grade				2.4	.5 ⎰	
Vocational Ed.	9.5	5	14.5	14.5	2.7	
TOTALS			167.538	528.705		

[1]Teacher Units
[2]See p. 216 for calculation method.

Appendix P *(Con't.)*

CERTIFIED PERSONNEL

STAFFING CHART

	Classroom	Kdg.	Reading	Library	Spec. Ed.	Counseling	Art Music Phys. Ed.
Elementary							
Arlington	20	2	1	1			2.1
Baird	20	2	1	1			2.4
Central	8	0	.5	.5			1.2
Farrow	16	1.5	1	1	3		2.1
Fisher	18	2.5	1	1			2.1
Gensimer	16	1	1	1		.5	1.8
George	2	0					.6
Isaacs	17	2	1	1	1-help		1.8
Mentor	16.5	2.5	1	1	1-help		1.8
Sunderland	15	1	1	1			1.5
Sylvan	10	1	.5	.5		.5	1.2
Tarrow	9	1	.5	.5			.9
Taylor	0	2					
Total = 230.5	167.5	18.5	9.5	9.5	5	1.0	19.5
Middle School							
East	24		1	1		1	
North	30.5		1	1		1	
West	27		1	1	2	1	
South	25.5		1	1		1	
Total = 121	107		4	4 ·	2	4	
High School							
Lincoln	146.5		3	4	2	9	
Washington							
Total = 164.5	146.5		3	4	2	9	

P.P.S.

Pupil Pers. Serv. 11

TOTALS 527=	432	18.5	16.5	17.5	9	14	19.5

Illus. 9-1

Appendix P *(Con't.)*

NON-CERTIFIED PERSONNEL

STAFFING CHART

	Secretaries	Custodians	Cooks	Teacher Aides	Lib. Aides	Cross. Gds.	Bus. Drivers	Mechanics	Nurses	Bookkeepers / Office Managers	Lunchroom Supv.	Bus Loading Supv.	Playground Supv.	Co-op
Elementary														
Arlington	1	4	2	.5	1	2					1	1	1	
Baird	1	4	3	2	1	2					1	1	1	
Central	1	3.1	1.5	1	1						1	1	2	
Farrow	1	4	2	2	1	1					1	1	2	
Fisher	1	4	3	1	1	1					1	1		
Gensimer	1	3.5	2		1	1					2	1	2	
George												5		
Isaacs	1	4	3	1	1						1	1	2	
Mentor	1	3.5	2	.5	1	2					1	1	2	
Sunderland	1	3.5	2	1	1	3					1		1	
Sylvan	1	3	1.5	.5	.5	3					1	.25	.25	
Tarrow	1	2.5	1.5	.5	.5	1					1	1	1	
Taylor						1								
Total	11	39.1	23.5	12	10	17					12	14.25	14.25	
Middle School														
East	3	9	3	2										
North	3	9	5	3							1			
West	3	9	5	4										
South	3	8.9	4.5	2	1						1		2	
Total	12	35.9	23.5	11	1						2		2	
High School														
Lincoln	10	22	10	8	2									6
Washington	6	18	6	4	2									3
Total	16	40	16	12	4									9
Central Office	15.6	5								2				1
Transportation	1						48	3						
Adult Education	1													
Detached	1													
Pupil Pers. Serv.	2								3					
GRAND TOTAL	59.6	120	57	35	15	17	48	3	3	2	14	14.25	16.25	10

Illus. 9-2

AN ALTERNATE METHOD OF COMPUTING FROM LEVEL I FUNCTION-OBJECT LINE BUDGET TO LEVEL II PROGRAM BUDGET AND LEVEL III BUILDING BUDGET BY PROGRAM

Appendix P displays teacher unit (TU) distribution by program and school. If you want to review this concept, a detailed description of teacher units and its derivation may be found in Chapter 2. This appendix describes an alternate method to that developed in Chapter 2, and is used to arrive at percentages to apply to the Level I function-object budget and to develop the Level II program budget. It can also be used to develop Level III building budgets from the Level II program budgets described in Chapter 3. It has the disadvantage of being more complicated to construct; however, it has the advantages of being more accurate, forms a better overall display of essential variables, and can form the basis for finer refinement and allocation of teacher units (TU).

The process requires allocating teacher time to Level II program analysis and Level III building cost analysis at elementary, middle school, and high school levels as displayed in Appendix P. The middle schools and high schools in Appendix P were separated for analysis by school, thus eliminating one series of calculations at the middle and high school levels. However, they could have been treated as a total district-wide block of grades 6-8 and 9-12, as the elementary schools were, if so desired. Since there is a large number of elementary schools in the district used in the example, they were treated as a block for convenience of calculation, and later separated by school by reallocating total teacher units.

In larger districts with greater numbers of middle and high schools, the application of this block approach with a second step separation, used with the elementary schools in the example that follows, would be easier to handle.

Computation of Level III Building Share of Budget

The elementary schools were separated by use of the following computations to arrive at Level III building cost analysis:

Computation 1

Arlington Elementary (1-5) total certified staff	24.1[1]
Arlington Elementary (1-5) total non-certified staff	13.5[1]
Arlington Staff Total	37.6

---

[1]Less Kindergarten since this is a separate program. Numbers based upon staffing charts that follow in this appendix.

Appendix Q *(Con't.)*

Computation 2

Total Elementary (1-5) certified staff	230.5
Total Elementary (1-5) non-certified staff	162.1
Elementary Total	392.6

Computation 3

Arlington Elementary (1-5) percent of total elementary (1-5) staff
$37.6 \div 392.6 = .09577 = 9.58\%$

Computation 4

Arlington Elementary % of total elementary (1-5) staff × total elementary program TU (teacher units) = Arlington Elementary share of TU (teacher units)

$$.0958 \times 240.011 = 22.99 \text{ TU}$$

Computation 5

Total budget ÷ Arlington Elementary share of TU (teacher units) = cost of operation of grades 1-5 at Arlington elementary

$$\$13,000,000 \div 22.9 = \$567,685.59$$

This process is repeated for each elementary school and provides total building operational cost per building.

Computation of Level II Program Share of Total Budget

Percentages to compute program share of total budget are arrived at by dividing program total TU (teacher units) by total TU (teacher units) for all K-12 programs. Thus, from the teacher unit distribution table, we arrive at the cost of the Art Program by the following method:

Total 1-5 Art TU (teacher units) ÷ Total K-12 TU (teacher units) = % of total program

$$26.525 \div 528.705 = .05016 \text{ or } 5.02\% \text{ (rounded to hundredths)}$$

When 5.016% is applied to a total budget of $13,000,000 we arrive at $652,080.

Appendix Q *(Con't.)*

Adjustments

Adjustments to the TU (teacher units) matrix may be made as often as necessary; however, unless major variations are made to the programs, the percentage distribution changes very little and therefore allows for rapid calculation of costs and distribution as estimated budget figures are needed.

Calculation of Community Service Budget

The total Community Service budget is $26,000, a small but rapidly increasing cost in many school districts.

Based upon 5 grades at elementary (5/12), 3 grades at middle school (3/12), and 4 grades (4/12) at high school level, this works out to $11,440, $6,240 and $8,320. These figures are then subjected to multiplication by the direct cost of the Community Services program attributable to each organizational level to convert them to equivalent TU (teacher units) for analysis.

This same analysis can be used for other similar program conversion to TU (teacher units).

APPENDIX R

INSTANT "CAS"
FILL IN THE BLANK FOR "CAS"

Line Item Budget	CAS Programs	CAS Program Budget	CAS Building Budget	CAS Grade Level Budget	CAS Subject Budget	CAS Teacher Unit Percentages
1.						
2.						
3.						
4.						
5.						
6.						
7.						
8.						
9.						
10.						
11.						
12.						
13.						
14.						
TOTAL						

Once these blanks are filled in correctly your CAS System is complete. All efforts should be made to maintain accuracy and completeness throughout the process of calculating this information.

Index